Lecture Notes in Computer Science 500

Edited by G. Goos and J. Hartmanis

Advisory Board: W. Brauer   D. Gries   J. Stoer

Martin Held

On the Computational Geometry of Pocket Machining

Springer-Verlag
Berlin Heidelberg New York
London Paris Tokyo
Hong Kong Barcelona
Budapest

Series Editors

Gerhard Goos
GMD Forschungsstelle
Universität Karlsruhe
Vincenz-Priessnitz-Straße 1
W-7500 Karlsruhe, FRG

Juris Hartmanis
Department of Computer Science
Cornell University
Upson Hall
Ithaca, NY 14853, USA

Author

Martin Held
Universität Salzburg, Institut für Computerwissenschaften und Systemanalyse
Jakob-Haringer-Straße 5, A-5020 Salzburg, Austria

CR Subject Classification (1991): I.3.5, I.3, E.1, J.6

ISBN 3-540-54103-9 Springer-Verlag Berlin Heidelberg New York
ISBN 0-387-54103-9 Springer-Verlag New York Berlin Heidelberg

Printing and binding: Druckhaus Beltz, Hemsbach/Bergstr.
2145/3140-543210 - Printed on acid-free paper

To describe right lines and circles are problems,
but not geometrical problems. The solution of
these problems is required from mechanics,
and by geometry the use of them, when so solved,
is shown; and it is the glory of geometry that,
from those few principles brought from without,
it is able to produce so many things.

(Isaac Newton's preface to *Principia*, 1686)

Foreword

We present a computational geometry approach to handling various problems arising from NC pocket machining. Our approach deals with practical as well as theoretical problems and links two scientific disciplines – computational geometry and mechanical engineering. Topics of practical importance that are dealt with include the selection of tool sizes, the determination of tool paths for contour-parallel and direction-parallel milling, and the optimization of tool paths. Seen from a practical point of view, we give full details of our algorithms (including implementational issues).

This practice-minded approach is embedded into a rigorous theoretical framework enabling us to state concise definitions and to prove the correctness and efficiency of our algorithms. In particular, the construction of Voronoi diagrams and their use for offset calculations are investigated in great detail. Based on Voronoi diagrams we introduce a graph-like data structure ('monotonous areas') that serves as a high-level abstraction of the pocket geometry and provides the basis for algorithmically performing shape interrogation and path planning tasks.

Our investigation is presented within three parts, each of which consists of a number of chapters. As far as possible we have tried to support selective reading, i.e. each part can be read without having to read the rest of the book. Where necessary, references are given to ideas and terms explained in other chapters.

In Part I we start with a comprehensive survey of our work and the results obtained. This part does not require a deeper understanding of concepts and ideas of computational geometry or CAD/CAM. On the contrary, Chap. 1 presents an easy-to-understand introduction to these fields of interest. In addition, an informal specification of the pocket machining problem is given and the prior work of other authors is reviewed. The next two chapters, Chaps. 2 and 3, highlight the main aspects of our work on contour-parallel and direction-parallel milling for pocketing. Part I is concluded by Chap. 4, which states our notational conventions and recalls definitions of common terms frequently used in this book.

Part II deals with contour-parallel milling for pocketing. Chapter 5 presents the underlying theory for constructing Voronoi diagrams of the boundaries of simply-connected and multiply-connected planar areas. Chapter 6 gives detailed information on implementational issues of Voronoi diagrams. In Chap. 7, we introduce our concept of monotonous areas. Chapter 8 concludes this part by applying the theory elaborated in the previous chapters to the actual generation of the tool path for contour-parallel milling.

Part III consists of two chapters on direction-parallel milling. Chapter 9 starts by introducing the mesh, which is a high-level abstraction of the pocket and tool path geometry and is used for zigzag path planning. Chapter 10 presents the actual generation of the tool path for direction-parallel milling. This task is carried out by working entirely on the precomputed mesh.

Finally, in the appendix some sample pocketing examples are plotted. These pockets have been processed by our own implementation of our algorithms for contour-parallel and direction-parallel milling and illustrate the power and efficiency of the concepts introduced.

Acknowledgements

This book is a revised version of my doctoral dissertation accepted by the Departments of Mathematics and Computer Science at the University of Salzburg (Salzburg, Austria). I owe a lot of thanks to all those who have contributed to my thesis.

In particular, I am grateful to H. Persson (SAAB-SCANIA AB, Linköping, Sweden) for the initial support of my work. He has significantly influenced my research by providing me with information about machining practice and by commenting on my suggestions in great detail.

I acknowledge the valuable discussions and exchange of ideas with A. Bodner (AIS GesmbH, Linz, Austria), G. Geise and D. Kochan (Technical U. Dresden, FRG), G. Lukács and T. Várady (MTA SZTAKI, Budapest, Hungary), K. Preiss (Ben-Gurion U. of the Negev, Beer-Sheva, Israel), and with W. Purgathofer (Technical U. Vienna, Austria). They also served as external referees of my thesis and helped to improve its presentation by their comments.

The major part of the underlying work for my thesis was carried out during my stay at the Research Institute for Symbolic Computation (RISC-Linz, U. of Linz, Austria). I remember a number of inspiring discussions with members of RISC-Linz. In particular, I would like to thank B. Buchberger, the chairman of RISC-Linz, for his efforts to teach me the basics of scientific working.

Finally, I am thankful to my advisors, J. Linhart and H.D. Clausen, for encouraging my work and for giving me the possibility to devote most of my time to writing this thesis.

Salzburg, March 1991   M. Held

Contents

II Contour-parallel Milling

Part I

Survey

Chapter 1

Introduction

1.1   Computational Geometry

The term 'Computational Geometry' originates from an (unpublished) manu-
script of Shamos and has become known after the publication of his Ph.D. thesis
[Sha78]. Preparata and Shamos' textbook [PS88] finally helped to establish it
among a large number of scientists. Besides[1], a group of researchers doing work on
the geometric modeling of curves and surfaces has also referred to their discipline
as 'Computational Geometry', cf. Forrest [For71]. Recently, in [For87a], Forrest
has distinguished between 'Theoretical Computational Geometry' (à la Shamos)
and 'Practical Computational Geometry' (i.e. his own research contribution).
Anyway, originally separated from each other, both research areas seem to be
undergoing a unification. Furthermore, the connections to combinatorial and
algebraic geometry are strengthened.

    'Theoretical computational geometry' as an independent area of research has
emerged in the early seventies of this century. Problems studied in the early
days include Euclidean traveling salesman, minimum spanning tree, hidden line,
and linear programming problems. Recently, however, a more systematic study
of geometric algorithms has been carried out, and a fast growing number of
scientists has been attracted to this discipline.

    Theoretical computational geometry deals with the design and analysis of
algorithms handling geometric entities (such as points, lines, hyper-planes, etc.).
During the last decade, besides worrying about the correctness of algorithms, the
analyses carried out have been mainly concerned with the worst-case behaviour
of algorithms. This approach is inherited from classical algorithm theory.

    Only recently, a trend towards designing algorithms that achieve a good
average-case complexity can be noted. Average-case analysis is of an enormous
practical importance because the algorithm most suitable for practical sizes of
input is not necessarily the asymptotically optimal one. Anyway, one of the major
outcomes of computational geometry is the general acceptance that some of the
traditional characterizations of geometric entities are inadequate for obtaining
'fast' and 'efficient' algorithms, no matter which meaning of 'fast' and 'efficient'
is considered.

    Throughout this book, we will make extensive use of data structures and algo-
rithms attributed to theoretical computational geometry. Hence, to some extent
our investigation is carried out in the original sense of Preparata and Shamos.
However, we are not only interested in isolated algorithms. Rather, the goal has
been to draw up a whole geometric system that *does* work and that can be used
in daily applications. Consequently, we have adopted a more pragmatic attitude
towards worst-case efficiency. Furthermore, we have put particular emphasis on

---

[1]Additionally, the term 'Computational Geometry' has been used as a subtitle by Minsky
and Papert in their landmark book [MP69].

the handling of special cases that constitute the bugbear of actual implementations of geometric algorithms. In addition, we are dealing with problems caused by numerical inaccuracy. Hence, following Forrest's terminology, the term 'computational geometry' in the title of our book can and should also be interpreted as 'practical computational geometry'.

We will give reference to prior and related work on specific aspects of (theoretical) computational geometry at appropriate points. General introductions to this area of interest are provided by the textbooks of Mehlhorn [Meh84c], Edelsbrunner [Ede87], and Preparata and Shamos [PS88]. Toussaint has edited a collection of papers addressing different (and separate) aspects of computational geometry, cf. [Tou85]. A quick reference to computational geometry has been published by Lee and Preparata in [LP84]. Additionally, as a further source of information on up-to-date research results, the proceedings of ACM Siggraph's Annual Conference on Computational Geometry and Springer Verlag's quarterly journal on Discrete & Computational Geometry have to be cited.

1.2 NC Pocket Machining

1.2.1 Introduction to NC Milling

Among the different kinds of metal cutting shaping, milling holds a predominant position in manufacturing practice. Roughly, a milling cutter can be considered as a cylindrical object rotating around its axis of symmetry. As illustrated in Fig. 1.1 moving a milling cutter on a billet produces a slot. Mathematically, this material removal can be regarded as subtracting the volume of the tool swept from the billet.

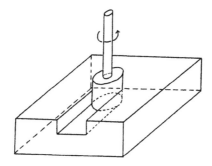

Figure 1.1: Basic Aspects of Milling.

The predominant position of milling is due to its wide range of industrial applications. As long as a final shape has to be produced from an initial shape by means of material removal, milling is chosen as the natural way of manufacturing. Possible applications comprise cutting a simple slot as well as preparing an injection mould or manufacturing turbine blades for power stations.

Of course, it makes a difference whether a simple planar slot or a complex three dimensional blade has to be manufactured. In the case of the slot it may be sufficient to drive the tool along straight lines in a horizontal plane whereas manufacturing turbine blades makes it necessary to move the cutter along spatial curves thereby obeying a number of additional restrictions. These differences are reflected by the various types of NC machines utilized in practice, on one hand, and by the different schemes of tool path control, on the other hand.

Basically, an NC[2] machine consists of a worktable, a spindle and several axes for positioning the tool and/or the worktable (together with the motors and controls for driving the axes). Typically, up to three axes are translational axes, corresponding to the three axes of a Cartesian coordinate systems. Additional axes are revolute ones supporting inclinations of the coordinate system. For a classical introduction to NC we refer to Bézier [Bez70].

1.2.2 Main Types of NC Path Control

According to the number of axes controllable simultaneously and independent of each other, one distinguishes between the following concepts for NC path control (cf. Fig. 1.2):

2D continuous-path control: It enables controlling two (translational) axes. Thus, 2D path control supports only planar milling applications. Normally, correlation schemes of the two axes are restricted to linear and circular interpolation.

3D continuous-path control: It enables linear interpolation using all three translational axes simultaneously. Any circular interpolation can only take place in one of the coordinate planes (i.e. xy-, yz- or xz-plane). Furthermore, helical interpolation is often supported. Parabola interpolation is sometimes included, too.

5D continuous-path control: Additionally to the features of 3D milling, two further axes of rotation are controllable. Hence, the simultaneous movement in three axes can be accompanied by a simultaneous rotation of the turntable and a swiveling of the tool mounting. As any milling machine is equipped with a spindle (giving the third axis of rotation), milling machines under 5D path control provide three translational and three rotational axes.

---

[2]During the last years, the concept of 'numerical control' (NC) has been gradually replaced by a concept making more directly use of a computer: 'computerized numerical control' (CNC). In our book, we do not distinguish between them. Rather, we use the term 'NC' synonymously for any of the two concepts.

It is well-known that six degrees of freedom are necessary and sufficient in order to be able to approach any spatial point with any required orientation (within reasonable limits of reach, cf. Paul [Pau81]). Thus, 5D path control is especially well-suited for the accurate machining of complex mechanical parts bounded by double-curved surfaces (e.g. blades, car bodies, turbines, vanes). Besides the gain in accuracy, productivity is also increased because there are no delays needed for repositioning the part as in the case of 3D path control.

Typical resolutions of NC controls for milling lie in the range of $10^{-2}mm$ to $10^{-4}mm$. As an abbreviation, the term 'milling under αD path control' is usually abridged to 'αD milling'.

The major drawback of 5D milling (and, to a smaller extent, of 3D milling) is its need of accurate control data for the simultaneous control of several motion axes. Apart from these programming difficulties, the same problems arise as in the fields of robotics. Detecting and avoiding collisions between the tool and its mounting, on one hand, and the workpiece, on the other hand, reveals subtle mathematical and algorithmical problems (still waiting for practicable solutions). Hence, when using 5D milling there exists a persistent danger of part or tool damage. Besides, representation and visualization of the in-process part geometry becomes rather complicated.

Due to these problems, 5D milling is only used if there is no way around. On the other hand, 2D milling suffers from a series of drastic restrictions that prevent it from being a practicable alternative to 5D milling. This gap between practical requirements, on one hand, and programming deficiencies, on the other hand, is closed by a hybrid form of 2D milling and 3D milling: $2\frac{1}{2}\mathbf{D}$ **milling** (cf. Fig. 1.2). Using $2\frac{1}{2}D$ path control, three dimensional milling is possible in principle. But there exists a restriction concerning the supported interpolations. As in the case of circular interpolations of 3D path control, any linear interpolation can only be carried out after one of the coordinate planes has been selected as an interpolation plane. This means that only two axes are continuous-path controlled whereas the third axis is point-to-point or straight-line controlled.

1.2.3 Motivation for Pocket Machining

The majority of industrial milling tasks can be performed using $2\frac{1}{2}D$ milling. According to Harenbrock [Har80], more than 80% of all mechanical parts to be machined can be cut by applying this concept for path control. This is partially due to the following two facts:

1. A surprisingly large number of mechanical parts is 'terrace-shaped', i.e. their boundary faces are either parallel to the xy-plane or constantly nor-

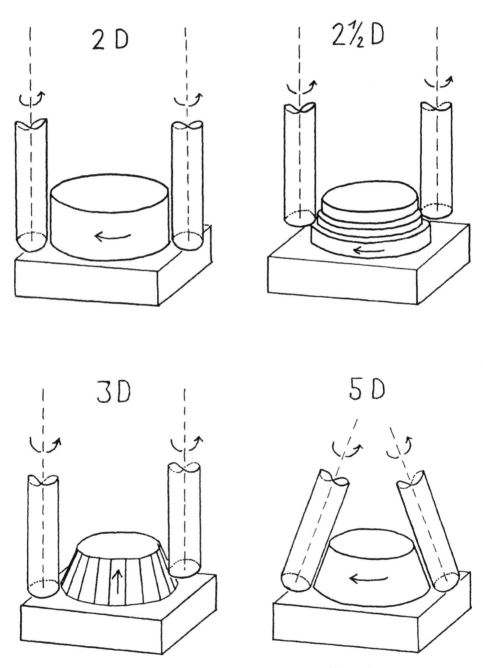

Figure 1.2: Main Types of NC Path Control.

mal on the xy-plane. By convention, such objects are usually called $2\frac{1}{2}$-dimensional.

2. More complicated objects – such as goal shapes bounded by free-form surfaces – are usually produced from a billet by $2\frac{1}{2}$D roughing and 3D–5D finishing. This means that a terrace-like approximation of the goal shape is produced in a first production step in order to clear away major concentrations of excess material.

Hence, the algorithmic handling of complex $2\frac{1}{2}$D milling tasks is of fundamental importance in order to be able to use this technologically simple approach to its utmost limits.

It is not trivial to suggest suitable z-levels of the layers for applying the roughing cuts (for item 2 of the above list). Besides sticking to minimal and maximal cutting heights (imposed by the machine tool under use), it is worthwhile to try to obtain a sufficiently good approximation of the goal shape thereby minimizing the number of resulting intersection curves between the goal shape and the different z-planes.

1.2.4 Informal Problem Specification

For the following it makes no difference in which way the machining levels have been obtained: machining takes place in different planes (parallel to the machining plane) cutting planar areas. Hence, by means of the $2\frac{1}{2}$D approach, the dimensionality of the underlying machining space can be reduced from 3D to $2\frac{1}{2}$D and finally to 2D.

The success of this approach highly depends on the availability of efficient algorithms for milling the resulting planar areas. This milling problem is known as *Pocket Machining Problem* and can be informally specified as follows:

Given: 1) Boundary contours enclosing a multiply-connected planar area (pocket),
             2) the size of a tool.

Determine: Tool path for machining the pocket.

The corresponding $2\frac{1}{2}$D machining process is depicted in Fig. 1.3.

1.2.5 Machining Strategies

Known approaches to pocketing can be distinguished by the milling strategy and by the way the cutter path is constructed according to such a strategy. Whereas the generation of the cutter path seems to differ from algorithm to algorithm

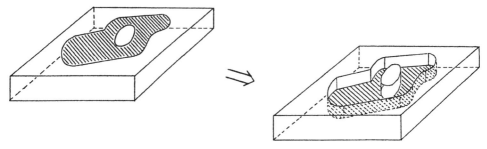

Figure 1.3: Pocket Machining.

there exist only two types of milling strategies. It is obvious that any algorithm cannot avoid driving the cutter along the contours in a first (last, respectively) pass. As depicted in Fig. 1.4, the areas remaining uncut are machined using one of the following strategies:

- contour-parallel milling,

- direction-parallel milling.

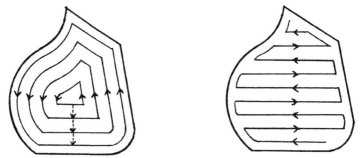

Figure 1.4: Contour-parallel and Direction-parallel Milling.

Contour-parallel milling uses offset elements (of the pocket contour) as cutter path elements. This means that the pocket area is milled in a spiral-like fashion cutting along curves equidistant to the contour and stepping outwards (inwards, respectively) for the next pass. These passes are computed similarly to the out-most one used for milling along the contour. As offset curves are used for milling, this strategy also came to be known as offset (curve) milling or window frame milling.

The basic idea of direction-parallel milling – also known as zigzag[3], stair case, hatch, or lacing milling – is apparently simple: after selecting an initial

---

[3]We will freely mix the terms offset (zigzag, respectively) milling and contour-parallel (direction-parallel, respectively) milling.

reference line milling takes place using line segments parallel to this reference line as cutter path elements. Zig milling is derived from zigzag milling by replacing the sequence of alternate left-to-right and right-to-left movements by a sequence of only left-to-right (right-to-left, respectively) movements. Its main advantage over true zigzag milling is the fact that cutting alternately with and against the spindle direction is avoided. Using zig milling, the tool cuts either only with the spindle direction – so-called conventional milling – or only against the spindle direction – so-called climb milling, cf. Fig. 1.5. Usually, zig milling gives a better surface quality. However, the number of tool retractions is significantly larger than in the case of true zigzag milling because the tool has to be lifted after each single zig move.

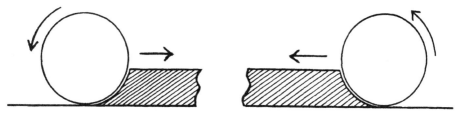

Figure 1.5: Conventional and Climb Milling.

1.3 Analysis of Prior and Related Work

1.3.1 Remarks on NC Part Programming for Pocketing

Following Groover and Zimmers [GZ84], numerical control part programming 'is the procedure by which the sequence of processing steps to be performed on the NC machine is planned and documented'. Basically, there are two methods of part programming: manual part programming and computer-assisted part programming. However, the manual preparation of control data requires a great deal of personal skill, imaginative ability in three dimensions, technological knowledge, and accuracy. Obviously, manual part-programming may become an extremely tedious task subject to various human errors.

Thus, software for computing the required control data plays an important role in order to utilize the full capacity of today's manufacturing computers and NC machines up to their utmost limits. During the last decades, a major goal has been the development of NC programming languages in order to simplify the part programmer's task. Starting with the initial MIT research on NC programming in the mid-fifties, some hundred NC part programming languages have been developed. Well-known representatives are given by MIT's original 'Automatically Programmed Tools' (APT) and its derivatives such as the German-developed

'EXtended subset of APT' (EXAPT), cf. Rembold and Dillmann [RD86], Kral [Kra86].

Basically, an APT-like language comprises four types of statements:

Definition Statements: Define the part geometry. They are sometimes called 'geometry statements'.

Motion Statements: Define the cutter path.

Postprocessor Statements: Specify machine- and task-dependent control values such as feed rates.

Auxiliary Statements: They are miscellaneous statements for specifying tolerances, etc.

In order to obtain the cutter path, the part programmer has to specify the required tool motion with respect to the part geometry. For instance, in order to drive the tool along one side of a profile, it is sufficient to indicate the profile and the required offset. The actual computation of the offset path is executed by the APT programming system. This contouring capability is based on the concept of using a so-called part surface, a drive surface, and a check surface, cf. Groover and Zimmers [GZ84]. The underlying idea is to drive the tool, with its side tangential to the drive surface and its bottom on the part surface, until the check surface is reached.

Furthermore, so-called macros – resembling procedures of modern programming languages – may be used for expressing motion statements that would be repeated several times within one NC program. In addition, some languages offer the use of 'high-level' macros. They correspond to tasks frequently encountered in the manufacturing practice (such as pocketing).

1.3.2 State of the Art

These high-level macros usually suffer from rather restricted capabilities. For instance, when using the APT-enhancement 'Super-Pocket' as described by Lallande *et al* [L*84], large areas have to be overlapped by the part programmer in order to be able to handle pockets containing islands. Today's commercial pocketing systems are often either limited by restrictions concerning the permitted shape of the input area or by poor capabilities of supplying the user with technological data, cf. Wang *et al* [W*87]. Few systems are able to generate tool paths which obey to advanced optimization criteria.

Surprisingly there exist only few serious investigations of the pocketing topic, see the work of Grayer [Gra75], Persson's landmark paper [Per78], Bruckner's publication [Bru82], Diedenhoven's thesis [Die84], the artificial intelligence approach of Preiss and Kaplansky [PK83,PK85], [Pre89], the evaluation [W*87] by Wang *et al*, Hansen and Arbab's paper [HA88] on offsetting, and Guyder's report [Guy89] on important issues of pocketing. The academic research community seems to entirely concentrate on advanced multi-axis NC machining and NC verification. Furthermore, a growing number of researchers works on higher-level path planning by means of solid models and form features, see for instance the publications of Choi, Barash and Anderson [C*84,CB85], Parkinson [Par86], Genord *et al* [G*88], Yeh and Ying [YY88].

Pocket machining gives way to subtle algorithmic problems that caused much frustration among researchers. Quoting from Preiss [Pre89], 'pocketing includes many, very much more complex situations. It is for this reason, little discussed in the literature, that so few automatic pocketing computations succeed to solve all cases of pockets. For instance, the book [Woo86] by Woodward, discussing automatic offsetting, which is just a part of the automatic pocketing problem, mentions "Detecting and rectifying all these problems automatically is difficult to implement reliably"'.

During the last years we have tried to close this gap by investigating an algorithmic approach in order to build up a workbench of fast algorithms for different pocket machining applications. These algorithms have been implemented and tested, resulting in the program packages GEOPOCKET and ZIGPOCKET for a fully automatic generation of the tool path. Recent results have been documented in [Hel88,Hel89,Hel91]. Earlier publications include [Hel87a] and the author's diploma thesis [Hel87b].

As stated above, there exist only two different machining strategies but a wide variety of algorithms for computing the cutter path according to these two strategies. Roughly, the approaches to pocketing can be classified in the following four groups (according to the means they use):

- conventional or set theoretical approach,

- artificial intelligence approach,

- computational geometry approach,

- computer graphics approach.

Whereas the first three approaches aim at realizing contour-parallel milling, the last item constitutes an approach to direction-parallel milling. In the sequel, the first two approaches are explained in more detail. The rest is treated within the succeeding survey chapters on contour-parallel and direction-parallel milling.

1.3.3 Conventional or Set Theoretical Approach

Harenbrock [Har80], Bruckner [Bru82] and Diedenhoven [Die84] have described a straightforward approach to generating the tool path. The basic idea of their approach is to mill the pocket by successively shrinking its contours. We have named this approach 'set theoretical' because it uses means like union and intersection of areas.

Of course, the actual heart of this approach is the computation of offset curves. As described by Harenbrock [Har80] and Bruckner [Bru82], this task is executed by the following three steps, cf. Fig. 1.6:

1. For every contour element an elementary offset element is constructed.

2. Gaps between the offset elements (at non-tangential meetings of pocket contour elements) are closed by joining arcs. This results in some (perhaps self-intersecting) closed curves.

3. Self-intersections of the curves are eliminated and portions of the curves (that have a minimal distance to a contour less than the required offset) are cleared away yielding the final offset curve(s).

Figure 1.6: Conventional Offsetting.

The main problem with this approach is the need to determine all self-intersections. Up to now, no method has been investigated in order to avoid intersecting every pair of offset elements. Hence, the worst-case complexity of this approach cannot be better than quadratic in the number of offset elements, and this number is linearly related to the number of pocket contour elements. Therefore, we expect that frequent computations of offset curves will consume quite a lot of CPU-time when using this approach.

Besides, executing step 3 is a non-trivial task. Normally, first an initial start point is searched which is guaranteed to be a member of the final offset contour. Then a process called 'loop removal' is started. Its task is to remove the excess portions of the curves in order to obtain the final offset curves. However, the curves are only searched between consecutive intersection points. For a more detailed description we give reference to Bruckner [Bru82].

This scheme works well for pockets not containing islands. However, in the presence of islands it may fail totally. Consider the following example: A pocket is bounded by two concentric full circles with radii $\rho_1 < \rho_2$. Let $d := \rho_2 - \rho_1$ and consider offsetting by an offset $t := \frac{2}{3}d$. Obviously, steps 1 and 2 of the above algorithm generate two concentric circles. Unfortunately, these circles do not intersect although both circles would have to be cleared away.

In order to cope with this and similar problems, Hansen and Arbab [HA88] and Preiss [Pre89] have investigated complex theories. Due to lack of space, we do not present details of their algorithms.

1.3.4 Artificial Intelligence Approach

In the course of numerous research activities in the fields of Artificial Intelligence (AI) there has been some work devoted to the application of AI to machining operation planning. For instance, see the work of Descotte and Latombe [DL81,DL84], Hall and Putnam [HP84], Mayer *et al* [M*84]. In particular, Barkoczy and Zdeblick [BZ84] and Preiss and Kaplansky [PK83,PK85] have investigated AI approaches to pocketing.

The concept behind AI programs is that of operators which convert one state of the data (starting from an initial state) into another one in order to reach a goal state, cf. Nilsson [Nil80]. In our context a state is the data defining the status of the tool and of the part to be machined. An operation is a move of the tool changing the state of the data. In order to be able to solve the problem (i.e. to reach the goal state) one needs a sufficiently large collection of operators for converting the initial state through some intermediate states to the goal state. Also, and very importantly, one needs a logical structure which will decide in which order the operators have to be applied in order to solve the problem within reasonable CPU-time. It is common to define an evaluation function which represents a weighted cost of the solution.

Thus, from an artificial intelligence point of view the pocketing problem can be described as follows:

Given :

- An initial state (the raw material).
- A goal state (the part).
- A set of operators (i.e. machining rules such as 'Cut_Along_Edge').
- A control structure (i.e. technological knowledge) in order to be able to decide which operator can be applied.

- An evaluation function in order to find the solution that best meets some technological requirements.

Find :

- A sequence of operators that produce the part from the raw material (when performed on a milling machine). For the solution sequence the evaluation function should be minimal.
- Additional technological information such as speeds and feeds.

After a cutter has been selected, the machining rules are applied in order to get a sequence of machining operations for milling the pocket. These rules are based on standard machining practices such as minimizing the total number of passes. Embedded in the rules are variables, called 'technology parameters', whose numerical values may be modified in order to alter the system's performance. For instance, these parameters include the maximum allowable ratio of the cutter pass distance to the cutter diameter. Preiss and Kaplansky [PK85] suggest to make an AI machining program more efficient by conducting the search from the goal state (i.e. from the part) to the initial state (i.e. the raw material).

According to our experience AI programs tend to suffer from a high CPU-consumption if it is not possible to reasonably shortcut the search tree searched by those programs during program execution. In the fields of robotics, in order to solve path-finding and collision detection problems one tries to limit the number of reasonable robot movements by gaining more geometrical insight; we do not really understand how an explosive growth of possible tool movements can be avoided by means of simple rules (without explicitly solving underlying geometric problems).

It seems that the AI approach provides opportunities for productivity improvement by making technological knowledge available to a wide range of (unexperienced) users. For machining operation planning this aid could include strategies for the selection of the tool and for the determination of speeds and feeds. Furthermore, we believe that detecting and handling form features should be a promising area of application of AI approaches.

Chapter 2

Survey of Contour-parallel Milling

2.1 Introduction

2.1.1 Contents of the Chapter

We present a detailed description of an algorithm for $2\frac{1}{2}$D pocket machining by means of offsetting. The algorithm is capable of fully automatically computing the offset tool path for any multiply-connected planar area ('pocket') bounded by lines and circular arcs. To our knowledge, this book constitutes the first detailed publication of an offset machining algorithm for pocketing that needs no interactive supervision or verification.

The main aspect of our approach is to make extensive use of the concept of Voronoi diagrams. Based on Voronoi diagrams, we introduce a new data structure for supporting high-level planning of the machining path. After discussing these fundamentals we put our emphasis on explaining the solution of some advanced geometrical and technological problems inherently connected with offset machining (e.g. an automatic determination of optimal cutter pass distances).

2.1.2 Problem Specification

As motivated in the last chapter, when designing algorithms for controlling NC milling machines one has to tackle two main aspects: the determination of both, geometrical and technological data. In the particular case of pocketing we are solving the following problem:

Pocket Machining Problem (Offset Milling):

Given :

- boundary contours enclosing a multiply-connected planar area (a so-called 'pocket'),

- boundary contours of drilled holes and similar cavities,

- technological objectives and constraints.

Determine :

- suitable tool sizes (i.e. the size of a 'small' cutter for milling along the contours and of a 'large' cutter for machining the 'inner parts' of the pocket),

- a correct (and with respect to some criteria hopefully optimal) tool path for machining the pocket according to the technological requirements,

- the actual cutting width at every tool path segment (used for computing suitable feed rates),

- an estimation of the time needed for machining the pocket on an NC machine.

2.1.3 Restrictions Imposed on the Pocket

Throughout this chapter, we will assume that all island contours are contained in the interior of one border contour and that no pairwise intersection of the contours does occur. In order to have well-defined interiors we assume that all contours are oriented and closed curves and do not have coinciding edges or points of self-intersection. In mathematical terms this means that we deal with multiply-connected planar areas bounded by Jordan curves.

We restrict to contours consisting of straight line segments and circular arcs. This restriction is motivated by the fact that offsetting becomes a rather difficult task if curves containing elements other than lines and circular arcs are involved: Intersection routines for handling more general elements such as cubic splines become more difficult. In addition, these elements are not invariant under offsetting (e.g. the offset of a cubic spline is no longer a cubic spline). Thus, a complex mathematical machinery may be required, cf. Klass [Kla83], Tiller and Hanson [TH84], Hoschek [Hos85], Saeed *et al* [S*88a], Farouki and Neff [FN89].

Most NC machines are only capable of executing linear and circular interpolations. Consequently, any tool path not only consisting of lines and circular arcs has to be approximated before it can be fed into an NC machine.

For these two reasons, up to now it is common practice to approximate more complex curves by polygons or piecewise circular curves. Several algorithms for circular approximation have been published; see the work of Sabin [Sab77], Linhart and Stegbuchner [LS80], Geise, Harms and Langbecker [GH81,LG87], Marciniak and Putz [MP84], Rossignac and Requicha [RR87], Sharrock [Sha87].

Observe that no restriction is imposed on the number or global shape of the contours. This is of particular importance when dealing with complex-shaped pockets containing several islands. Such milling tasks frequently occur at aircraft industries, for instance.

2.2 Voronoi Diagrams and Offsetting

2.2.1 Motivation

One of the major problems when using a contour-parallel milling strategy is the need for performing difficult and time-consuming computations of offset curves. Usually, this task is executed in three steps by

1. elementary offsetting for each contour element,

2. closing gaps between the offset elements, and

3. eliminating self-intersections of the offset curves.

Such a conventional approach, as published by Bruckner [Bru82] and Hansen and Arbab [HA88], is capable of (or can, at least, be extended to) handling rather general contours consisting of different types of contour elements. But it seems not feasible if repeated computations of offsets of complex contours are required on a small-sized computer (such as a CNC computer). Besides, it is suspect to numerous computational problems, as stated by Preiss [Pre89].

Fortunately, in order to overcome this drawback, a completely different approach has been initiated by Persson in 1978. Dealing with simply-connected pocket areas, in his short but high-quality paper [Per78] he introduced the following idea: Pick out an arbitrary endpoint p of two consecutive cutter pass segments (cf. Fig. 2.1). Obviously, p has the same minimal distance from two contour elements and a greater distance from any other contour element.

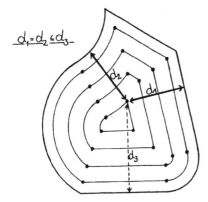

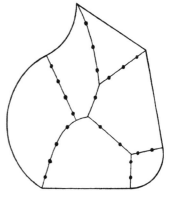

Figure 2.1: Elementary Property of Offset Points.

Figure 2.2: Voronoi Diagram.

Consider the set of points (in the interior of the pocket) that exhibit this property, cf. Fig. 2.2. In order to help intuition, imagine that a family of offset curves is constructed as follows: Starting with offset $d = 0$, d is continuously increased until the offset curve degenerates to a point (i.e. the contour is successively shrunk). One gets exactly the required set of points if one keeps track of the endpoints of the moving offset elements. In [PS88], Preparata and Shamos present a similar idea: Imagine that a prairie fire is applied simultaneously to all elements of the contour. Then one gets this set of points by taking the points where fire waves meet – supposed that the fire propagates at constant speed. It turns out that these points form a graph-like structure which is well-known in the fields of computational geometry as the Voronoi diagram defined by the contour elements.

Summarizing, the Voronoi diagram yields a planar subdivision of the pocket where each of the subareas corresponds to exactly one contour element. These subareas are commonly called 'Voronoi areas'. The border elements between two subareas (the so-called 'bisectors') are the loci of points that are equidistant to the two corresponding contour elements.

2.2.2 Using Voronoi Diagrams for Offsetting

What is the advantage of considering Voronoi diagrams when computing offset curves? One should observe that the availability of the Voronoi diagram considerably facilitates the construction of offset curves because it is sufficient to apply the above presented idea for defining the diagram in reverse order: the endpoints of a segment of an offset curve can be computed by

1. constructing the elementary offset segment of a contour element, and by

2. intersecting the elementary offset segment with the bisectors bounding the Voronoi area that corresponds to the defining contour element.

Supposed that a suitable representation of the Voronoi diagram is used, this algorithm can efficiently be executed. In particular, when expressing the bisectors as functions of their minimal distance[1] to the defining contour elements, the computation of these intersections can merely be reduced to simple evaluations of the bisector parameterization formulas, using the requested offsets as evaluation parameters. Thus, computing tool paths consisting of several passes (i.e. closed offset curves) is not that difficult when using Voronoi diagrams.

To our knowledge, we are the first who have picked up Persson's ideas and published (and implemented) a general concept for fully automated pocket machining. A similar approach is claimed by Spur *et al* [S*88c]. Unfortunately, we could not gain more information because our query letters have not been answered.

2.2.3 Constructing Voronoi Diagrams

In [Per78], Persson presents some rough ideas for constructing Voronoi diagrams of rather simply-shaped contours. Worst-case optimal algorithms for constructing Voronoi diagrams of sets of points and straight lines have been published by Kirkpatrick [Kir79], Lee [Lee82], Yap [Yap85,Yap87], and Fortune

---

[1]This has been suggested by Persson in [Per,Per78].

[For85,For86,For87b]. Except Fortune who has investigated a plane sweep technique, all the other authors use a divide-and-conquer technique in order to obtain the $O(n \log n)$ upper bound, where n denotes the total number of contour elements. Lee restricts to computing the Voronoi diagram of simple polygons whereas the other authors deal with general sites being arbitrarily scattered over the plane. In particular, they are able to handle multiply-connected areas bounded by simple polygons. In addition to points and lines, Yap's algorithm is able to handle circular arcs.

According to reasons explained in Chapter 5, we have decided to design and implement an own approach. Roughly, in the case of a simply-connected pocket we proceed as suggested by Lee. In the case of a multiply-connected pocket, Voronoi diagrams are computed for each of the single contours and incrementally merged together in order to obtain the final diagram. Chapter 5 presents full details. Recently, we have been informed that our approach is very similar to that of Srinivasan and Nackman, cf. [SN87].

For the following we suppose that an algorithm for constructing Voronoi diagrams is available.

2.3   Solving Geometrical Problems of Pocketing

2.3.1   Modifying the Pocket Contours

Due to technological considerations it sometimes may be reasonable to keep some margin at the boundary uncut. For instance, a special finishing pass might be applied. If the same margin is required to be kept uncut at all contours this can readily be achieved by adjusting the offset of the outmost cutter pass. In case that different margins are specified it is more convenient to individually enlarge (shrink, respectively) the contours by computing offset contours. This task can be performed by using the same technique as described above.

Apart from these user-requested modifications of the contours we are redefining the pocket contours by means of 'contour bridges' in order to simplify the generation of the tool path. As depicted in Fig. 2.3, we connect the island contours with the border contour. This is done at some points of minimal distance between the contours. Fortunately, candidates for these connection points can be computed from the Voronoi diagram by means of graph-search techniques. Afterwards, an Euclidean minimum spanning tree algorithm (cf. [PS88]) is applied to this set of candidates in order to determine the actual connection points.

As a matter of principle, any multiply-connected pocket area can be transformed to a simply-connected one by means of these joining line segments. But there will be an unexpected side-effect: even if the pocket area is totally milled with respect to the 'new' contour it may happen that small areas at the joining

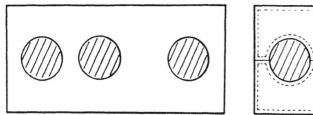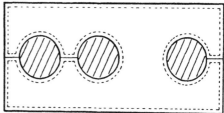

Figure 2.3: Redefining the Boundary.

line segments are left uncut (due to the use of regrinded cutters, for instance). Things get worse if it is required to keep a certain contour distance. In this case one cannot help leaving some bars uncut at the joining segments. Obviously, this is not optimal as our goal is to guarantee that the pocket area is totally milled with respect to the original contours.

In order to preserve tangent-continuity and to avoid leaving some bars uncut at the joining segments we construct the contour bridges[2] as depicted in Fig. 2.4: Choosing the radii of the joining circular arcs equal to the required contour distance of the outmost cutter pass ensures that the original multiply-connected pocket area is totally machined if the resulting simply-connected area[3] is totally machined.

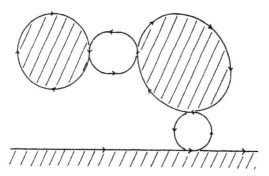

Figure 2.4: Close-up of a Contour Bridge.

Of course, the Voronoi diagram of the simply-connected pocket can be obtained from the original one by locally modifying the structure at the connection points. Furthermore, in general the construction of the contour bridges will not

---

[2] According to Persson [Per], a similar approach is used at SAAB/SCANIA.

[3] In strict mathematical terms the resulting pocket area should not be called 'simply-connected' because there exist some overlaps. In more precise terms this means that the contour of the transformed pocket area is homotop to the contour of a simply-connected area (such as a circle).

cause a dramatic increase of the total length of the tool path. Thus, for the rest of this chapter we can concentrate on simply-connected pocket areas.

2.3.2 The Concept of Monotonous Areas

Supposed that one is supplied with suitable cutter pass offsets, it has already been described by Persson [Per78] how to efficiently compute the tool path for a rather 'simple' pocket area (such as depicted in Fig. 2.2). In this simple case the tool path can be obtained by starting at the innermost point, milling along a cutter pass and by stepping outwards from this pass to the neighbouring outer pass.

However, the presence of straits (i.e. bottle-necks of the pocket contours) makes it impossible to cut the pocket in this spiral-like fashion by continuously stepping out from an inner cutter pass to the neighbouring outer pass. In order to overcome this difficulty, we introduce a subdivision of the pocket into subareas that can be milled more easily. It turns out that it is suitable to subdivide at straits of the pocket contours (cf. Fig. 2.5).

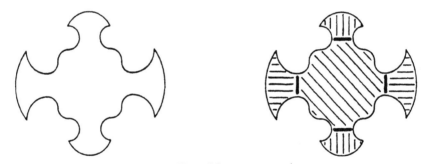

Figure 2.5: Five Monotonous Areas.

Observe that a pair of non-consecutive contour elements forms a strait if and only if these elements define a common bisector b and there exists one point p on b such that 'walking' away from p (along the Voronoi diagram) for an arbitrary small amount does not decrease the minimal distance to the contour. This property helps to find the straits in linear time $O(n)$ by means of standard graph search techniques.

We now subdivide the pocket area into subareas by straight line segments which connect corresponding contour elements of straits. Let us call a point 'innermost point' of such a subarea if no point of the area has a greater minimal distance to the contour. It is possible to prove that all innermost points have to be located on the Voronoi diagram. In particular, it is possible to prove that at least one node of the Voronoi diagram exhibits this property. Again by traversing the Voronoi diagram, the innermost points can be computed in linear time.

Moving away from an innermost point (along the Voronoi diagram towards the contour or towards a strait), the minimal distance to the contour will monotonously decrease. Due to this specific property we call these regions 'monotonous areas'. One should observe that monotonous areas need not be convex. However, monotonous areas can be milled in a spiral-like fashion as proposed by Persson.

Thus, based on the Voronoi diagram it is possible to draw up in linear time a graph-like data structure where

- every node corresponds to a monotonous area, and

- the incident edges correspond to straits separating this monotonous area from other areas.

With every node, the corresponding innermost point is associated. Besides, the metric informations concerning the contour offsets of the innermost points and the widths of the straits are provided. This data structure serves as a high-level abstraction of the shape of the pocket. In the sequel, we will make extensive use of this versatile structure.

For instance, the consideration of monotonous areas enables us to split up the complicated task of guaranteeing a totally milled pocket area into two subtasks: It is sufficient to ensure that each monotonous area is entered by the tool path if we are able to guarantee that each entered area will be totally milled. This fact is exploited in the next subsection when computing optimal pass distances.

Recently, we have been informed that Gürsoy and Patrikalakis [Gur89,PG90] have established a concept very similar to our monotonous areas and have successfully applied it to the generation of finite element meshes. However, in their approach the monotonous areas are not obtained from the Voronoi diagram. On the contrary, the Voronoi diagram is computed after all straits have been detected by a simple $O(n^2)$ algorithm.

2.3.3 Computing Optimal Cutter Pass Distances

In order to ensure total milling of a monotonous area the following problem has to be solved: given an inner cutter pass in a monotonous area, compute the locally optimal distance between this pass and the neighbouring outer cutter pass. In this context the term 'local' indicates that we restrict both cutter passes to the actual monotonous area without taking care of other areas.

As the optimal distance will always be less than or equal to the cutter diameter, no area can be left uncut between two 'parallel' offset elements of neighbouring cutter passes. However, choosing the pass distance equal to the cutter diameter possibly leaves some triangular-shaped areas uncut, cf. Fig. 2.6.

One can make sure that uncut areas are avoided if the pass distance is chosen equal to the cutter radius. Indeed, this is the way most pocket machining

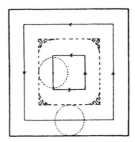

Figure 2.6: Uncut Triangular-Shaped Areas.

packages seem to handle this problem. Although there is no doubt that a uniform cutting width has its specific advantages, it is clear that one could save machining time by enlarging the pass distance. This is of particular importance when pocketing in soft material such as plastic foam, wood or even aluminium. Typically, about 70–80 percent of the diameter should be used as pass distance. Is there no way to do better?

One manner of tackling this problem is to directly mill towards the triangular area when moving along the inner pass as it has been suggested by Putz [Put], cf. Fig. 2.7. As this approach will likely produce rather short cutter path segments – which should be avoided according to Persson [Per] – and cause drastic changes of the milling direction – which might cause slowing down the NC machine – we did not persue this idea. Nevertheless, we would like to remark that details of a machining strategy can only be judged with respect to the actual requirements of some specific machine. Thus, there might exist applications where this approach seems to be perfectly right.

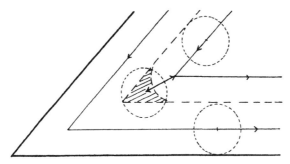

Figure 2.7: Putz's Suggestion.

In [Cze76b,Cze76a], Czeranowsky has proposed to compute a global upper bound on the cutter pass distances depending on the cutter radius ρ and the internal angle ϕ between pairs of consecutive contour elements, cf. Fig. 2.8. Restricting to line segments, straightforward calulations yield the bound $\rho + \rho \sin \frac{\phi}{2}$. But this formula may not be applied to circular arcs: this is due to the fact that the internal angles between consecutive contour elements, on one hand, and corresponding offset elements, on the other hand, are not equal. Besides, additional problems may arise.

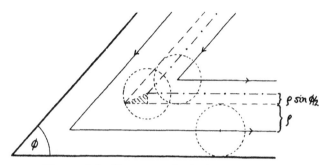

Figure 2.8: Czeranowsky's Approach.

Our way of handling the distance problem is to dynamically compute an optimal cutter pass distance between two passes. In this context 'optimal'[4] means that there is nothing left uncut between two passes and that this goal is not achieved if the distance would be chosen greater.

Let us call that point of the triangular shaped area which has the greatest minimal distance to the contour a *critical point*. It is easy to see that the critical point is situated on both, the Voronoi diagram and the circumference of the cutter circle centered at the common endpoint of the elements of the inner cutter pass, cf. Fig. 2.9. Furthermore, nothing is left uncut if the cutter circle covers the critical point when moving along the outer cutter pass.

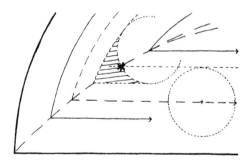

Figure 2.9: Covering the Critical Point.

Thus, we can state the following algorithmic approach to computing the optimal cutter pass distance within a monotonous area (cf. Fig. 2.10):

---

[4]In the section on 'technological aspects' we will refine this definition.

1. Center the cutter circle at the endpoints of elements of the inner pass and compute all intersections of the cutter circle with bisectors leading towards the contour.

2. Select that intersection point which has the greatest offset distance to the contour.

3. Subtract this distance from the offset of the inner pass and add the cutter radius.

Paying attention to special cases this algorithm yields the optimal cutter pass distance.

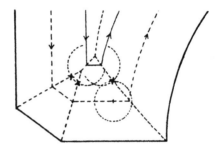

Figure 2.10: Computing an Optimal Cutter Pass Distance.

Normally, the computed pass distance will be in the range of the user-specified distance. However, the major disadvantage of our method – besides computational efforts – is the fact that the optimal pass distance may shrink to the cutter radius if sharp corners of the inner pass are involved. In order to avoid this effect it might be desirable to apply the method of Fig. 2.7 in such exceptional cases.

2.3.4   Generating the Tool Path

Having determined the optimal cutter pass distance, the generation of the tool path should be difficult no more. But there remains one problem unsolved: There likely will exist cutter passes that pass through more than one monotonous area. Thus, the computed cutter pass distances eventually have to be modified in order that each single pass has the same offset in each monotonous area. Obviously, any modification of the pass distances would destroy their optimality.

This is avoided by a simple trick. Instead of computing the pass distances and the tool path outwards in one step we split up the task into two subtasks: In the first step, we only compute the optimal cutter pass distances inwards. In a second step, the actual tool path is constructed outwards.

In more detail, we proceed as follows: Stepping inwards, the optimal distance between the outer pass and the next inner pass is computed[5] for each monotonous area. After sorting the monotonous areas according to these distance values the process of reducing some distances begins. Starting at that area which has the smallest optimal distance (i.e. the smallest corresponding contour offset), all the other monotonous areas that will be entered by a cutter pass at the resulting offset are determined (by means of the information on the monotonous areas) and their pass distances are set to the actual distance. Then the same process starts at that area with the smallest remaining distance.

By a repeated application of this scheme all distances between neighbouring cutter passes are determined no matter whether the passes enter several monotonous areas or whether they are only located in one area. Observe that the resulting pass offsets are optimal in the sense that they cannot be enlarged without leaving some areas uncut.

After the cutter pass distances (i.e. pass offsets) have been determined, it is no longer difficult to generate the final tool path thereby paying attention to the required milling direction. This merely means constructing offset curves (by means of the Voronoi diagram) and threading up the monotonous areas in the correct order.

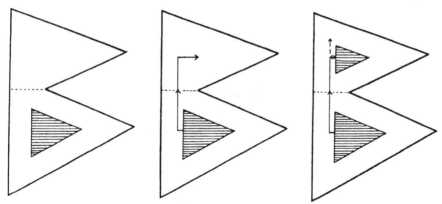

Figure 2.11: Recursively Generating the Tool Path.

As depicted in Fig. 2.11, the main idea is to mill a monotonous area until the tool passes through one of the area's straits and thus enters a new monotonous area. After milling towards the new area's inner point, the new area is machined until the 'old' offset is again reached. Then, the 'old' cutter pass continues. A recursive algorithm can be easily implemented for executing this task.

---

[5]Stepping inwards instead of outwards, the computation of the pass distances is a bit more difficult but conceptually not different from the algorithm described in the last subsection.

2.4   Pocketing Features of GEOPOCKET

Using the presented geometric tools – the Voronoi diagram and our concept
of monotonous areas, in particular – we are able to give efficient solutions to
the major geometrical and technological problems of pocketing. In more detail,
we have achieved the following outstanding features which make our package
GEOPOCKET a versatile tool for the practical machining of complicated mechanical parts.

2.4.1   Advanced Geometrical Features

- GEOPOCKET is able to fully automatically generate the tool path for machining any multiply-connected planar area (bounded by straight lines and
  circular arcs). Efficient machining is supported by its capability to use
  two different-sized cutters. The distance between two neighbouring cutter passes is dynamically optimized with respect to the geometrical and
  technological objectives[6].

- The powerful geometric concept of our method guarantees that the pocket
  is 'totally' milled, i.e. that any area which can be cut without violating
  any contour will be cut. Furthermore, it is ensured that no contour is
  damaged no matter how complicated the shape of the pocket is. On the
  contrary, if requested, it is possible to keep uncut different margins at the
  border and island contours. Thus, there is no need for a time-consuming
  and troublesome simulation and verification[7] of the tool path.

- GEOPOCKET executes some additional optimization tasks: As far as possible, pocket areas are not machined repeatedly and lifting the cutter and
  moving it in the air is avoided. Due to the second optimization criterion
  the number of holes is minimized that have to be drilled before milling can
  take place.

2.4.2   User Assistance and Advanced Technological Features

- GEOPOCKET enables a computer-aided tool selection: With respect to a
  user-specified corner coverage parameter it determines an upper bound for
  the admissible size of the cutter used for contour milling. Furthermore,

---

[6]The dynamic optimization with respect to technological objectives is constrained to 'quan-
tities with a geometric flavour', which can be expressed in geometrical terms. No attempt is
made to directly carry out optimizations with respect to other process parameters (such as the
material to be machined).

[7]As a matter of fact, NC programmers usually are hard to convince about this fact. They
tend to dislike actually running an NC program on an expensive machine tool *without* previously
having the computed tool paths displayed on a screen.

depending on this selected value and on the minimal width at straits of the pocket contours, a suitable size of the cutter applied for milling the 'inner parts' of the pocket is suggested.

- By specifying nominal and actual cutter diameters the user is able to handle possibly regrinded tools. Imposing minimal and maximal cutter pass distances gives the possibility to avoid overloading or underloading the tool. In this way, the generation of the tool path can be influenced in order to adapt the path to the actual requirements of the NC machine. By means of these restrictions on the cutter pass distances, one can easily control scallop heights if toroidal- or ball-ended cutters are to be used instead of flat-ended ones.

- For every cutter path segment the actual cutting width is computed. Thus, by computing optimal feed rates by means of evaluating information on the kind of material to be machined (which might be obtained from an AI module), tool breakage is avoided and a satisfying surface quality is ensured. The feeds together with the computed length of the cutter path can be used for obtaining a realistic calculation of the actual machining time on an NC machine.

- Drilled holes and similar cavities (i.e. regions of the pocket that have a surface lying below the actual machining level) can be automatically handled. By using rapid feed above these islands the cutting time may be considerably reduced. This is of particular importance when moulded work pieces have to be finished.

However, we emphasize that geometrical correctness and geometrical optimality of CAD/CAM programs are important issues but they are not the only issues that are of practical importance. In the particular case of pocket machining, it is perhaps equally important that an experienced NC programmer is able to override and alter computed data in order to modify the generation of the cutter path.

2.5 Solving Technological Problems of Pocketing

In this section we demonstrate how the geometric tools – the Voronoi diagram and the concept of monotonous areas, in particular – can be utilized for efficiently solving the stated technological problems. We do not claim that these technological objectives are the only ones being worth to consider. Rather, this section is intended to illustrate diverse possibilities for dealing with technological requirements within the introduced geometrical framework.

2.5.1 Computer-aided Tool Selection

Even if being concerned with a pocket area of simple shape it is not very easy
to select a suitable cutter size for machining. With increasing complexity of the
pocket or if two different-sized cutters should be used this rapidly becomes a
rather complicated task. Simply trying a series of cutter sizes by means of a
machining simulation can be avoided at least partially by using a geometrical
computer-aided tool selection. Depending on some user-specified control parameters, GEOPOCKET computes lower and upper bounds on the sizes of the cutters
and (together with some AI module using a data bank) it could select particular
tools, too.

For selecting a cutter used for finishing (i.e. milling along the boundary of
the pocket) one usually pays attention to the following three objectives:

1. The cutter should be able to pass through any narrow part of the pocket.
   Thus, taking the minimum of the widths at straits gives a reasonable upper
   bound on the cutter size.

2. If contours contain arcs it may be reasonable that the cutter is small enough
   in order to enable proper machining of each arc.

3. Contour elements enclosing an internal angle $< \pi$ cause special problems
   because it is not possible to exactly manufacture the resulting corners.
   Hence, some designers tend to à priori blend these corners by small arcs.
   Alternatively, specifying a corner coverage parameter is a good means for
   controlling the maximal extension of uncut corner regions.

Step 2) is easily performed by examining the minimal radii of curvature of the
contour elements. Trivially, in the case of a circular arc the minimal radius of
curvature is given by the arcs radius. The necessary distance information for carrying out steps 1) and 3) is readily available by using the computed information
on the Voronoi diagram and on the monotonous areas.

After fixing the size of the finishing cutter we are able to determine a suitable
size of a second cutter used for roughing (i.e. machining the 'inner' parts of the
pocket). Seen from a practical point of view, one would perhaps like to choose
a rather big cutter in order to be able to machine the pocket thereby needing
only few cutter passes. But the situation is not that simple because again uncut
triangular areas have to be avoided between the outmost pass (which is most
probably cut by a small-sized finishing cutter) and the neighbouring inner pass.

This problem differs from the problem of determining locally optimal cutter
pass distances because now the radius of the roughing cutter is unknown. Anyway, as depicted in Fig. 2.12, observe that the cutter radius ρ has to be $\geq d$ and
$\leq$ the contour offset t. By setting $d = t$ and solving the resulting equation for

t at each corner a set of 'locally' admissible cutter radii ρ is obtained. Taking the minimum of these values yields an upper bound on the size of the roughing cutter.

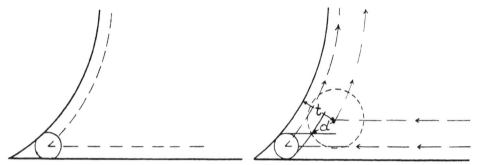

Figure 2.12: Upper Bound on the Size of the Roughing Cutter.

Again by means of the monotonous areas, the user is supplied with data on the widths of the straits of the pocket and on the offsets of the innermost points. Summarizing, using the Voronoi diagram it is quite easy to select suitable cutter sizes.

2.5.2 Ensuring a Satisfying Surface Quality

Control Parameters for Handling Different Cutting Tools

Up to this point we have regarded the cutter as a circle. Indeed, as every milling cutter is symmetric with respect to its rotation axis (being perpendicular to the machining plane), it is reasonable to treat the cutter as a circle. But according to Persson [Per], most cutters have a shape slightly differing from a cylinder. Instead of a sharp corner, a cutter normally has a fillet radius because

- the cutter tends to become brittle if it has a sharp corner,

- stress requirements usually make it necessary to have a corner radius between the pocket's bottom and the surrounding sides.

But there is an even more wide variety of cutting tools used in practice: various *special-shaped cutters* are used depending on the intended application.

Apart from the shape of the milling cutter there exists another problem arising from practice: Any cutter used for machining hard material for some time will not have its nominal size. Thus, one should be able to machine a pocket without leaving some areas uncut even if a smaller cutter is employed than that one used for the cutter path calculation. This means that a good pocketing package has to take care of an allowable interval for the cutter radius in order to be able to use regrinded tools.

GEOPOCKET *takes care of regrinded cutters* by regarding the regrinded radius as a user-specified percentage of the nominal radius yielding the so-called actual radius. This actual radius is utilized for coverage tests whereas the nominal radius is used for keeping a certain distance to the contours.

Beside the cutter size considerations, one also has to *avoid overloading* or *underloading the machining tool*. Underloading the cutter can cause non-cutting because the cutter may be bent away from the raw material (instead of cutting it) if the cutting width is too small. Overloading the cutter is no better policy as this can cause the cutter to jam and may result in a poor surface quality.

We tackle these problems by taking care of two user-specified control parameters, namely the minimal and maximal allowed cutter pass distances. This means that GEOPOCKET computes geometrically optimal pass distances and afterwards reduces/enlarges these distances if they should not be contained between the two bounds. One should observe that by influencing the cutting width the user is not only able to avoid underloading or overloading the tools but he also can easily control scallop heights resulting from the application of non-flat-ended tools.

Computing Optimal Feed Rates

Even if one takes care of a maximally allowed pass distance there will likely exist some segments of the cutter path where the actual cutting width is equal to the cutter's diameter. In particular, when stepping out from a pass to the neighbouring one or when passing through a strait this can hardly be avoided[8]. In order to ensure a sufficient surface quality it is necessary to reduce the feed rate at least at such cutter path segments.

GEOPOCKET meets this practical demand by computing the *actual cutting width* for each cutter path segment. As a first approach, one perhaps would suggest to obtain a rough approximation of the cutting width by taking the cutter pass distance. But this scheme can only be correctly applied if for every segment of the inner path there exists exactly one corresponding segment of the outer path and if the projections of such two path segments onto the defining contour element yield the same results. Otherwise, at the endpoints of the cutter path segments the cutting width will be larger than the cutter pass distance. On the other hand, at the innermost passes, driving the cutter along a path segment may cause a reduction of the cutting width for the segments lying on the opposite side of the actual bisectors with respect to the actual segment. Again, both problems are solved by keeping track of the endpoints of the segments of the last inner cutter pass and by using the Voronoi diagram for obtaining path segments lying on the opposite sides of certain bisectors.

---

[8]This can be avoided if tool retractions are considered less harmfull and the tool is allowed to be lifted and moved in the air, cf. Guyder [Guy89].

Summarizing, our geometric approach provides sufficient information for ensuring a good surface quality.

2.5.3 Further Technological Features

In addition to the above presented technological features, GEOPOCKET has two further capabilities: it takes care of negative islands and it tries to avoid short cutter path segments.

Handling Negative Islands

Taking care of negative islands means to check for each cutter path segment whether it is at least partially located above some area where machining is not necessary because its surface is lying completely below the machining level.

Suppose that a second Voronoi diagram as defined by the border contour and both positive and negative islands is available additionally to the diagram defined by the border contour and the positive islands. In order to avoid examining all negative islands for each cutter path segment – which might be quite a time-consuming task – it is useful to overlay both diagrams. Clearly a path segment does not pass over a negative island if both Voronoi diagrams contain identical informations at the relevant bisectors passing through the segment's endpoints. Otherwise, the path segment is in the neighbourhood of a specific contour element of a negative island. In this case we have to check by standard methods whether the segment intersects this contour element, i.e. whether the interior of the corresponding negative island is being entered.

Although this approach could still be improved we believe that it should be sufficient for the practical application of GEOPOCKET because usually the number of complex negative islands is rather small. Hence, handling negative islands can be accomplished within reasonable CPU-time by making use of Voronoi diagrams.

Avoiding Very Short Cutter Path Segments

According to Persson [Per], very short cutter path segments should be avoided because an NC machine has a minimum block handling time for each block. If this handling time is longer than the time needed for machining, then the NC machine has to slow down completely. Thus, a number of very short path segments may cause the tool to become stationary which usually gives poor surface quality.

There are several heuristic approaches to this problem. We use the following idea (due to Persson [Per]): In the case that during computing the cutter pass distances a very short path element occurs, the actual pass distance is reduced by a small amount. However, we must admit that there might be some problems if this strategy should cause a repeated adjusting of the distance.

Ensuring Sharp Corners at Reflex Vertices

Usually it should be avoided that the cutter has contact with the same area of the pocket several times. Machining around a reflex vertex – i.e. a corner with internal angle $> \pi$ – along the outmost cutter pass thereby following a circular arc centered at the vertex will not yield a sharp corner.

It is better to proceed as depicted in Fig. 2.13. By using the distance informations provided by the Voronoi diagram we are able to ensure that machining along the additional path segments does not cause a violation of the pocket boundary.

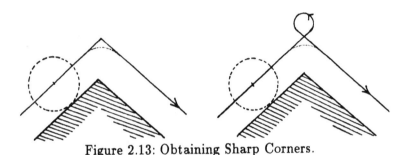

Figure 2.13: Obtaining Sharp Corners.

2.6 Concluding Remarks

In this chapter, we have presented an overall description of our pocketing package GEOPOCKET. Summarizing we can state its main features as follows: The package is able to handle any multiply-connected pocket area (limited by straight lines and circular arcs) thereby using two different-sized cutters. Besides, there is no need for visually verifying the computed tool paths. Solving a lot of technological problems, our approach meets most practical requirements of the shop floor.

We have achieved extremely fast computations. For instance, on a VAXstation 2000 running VMS, the CPU-time of about 200 tested examples has always been in the range of 1 to 20 seconds. For most practical applications the CPU-consumption will be considerably less than 10 seconds. A considerable speed-up can be obtained by computing the Voronoi diagram in a preprocessing step. For sample examples, we refer to the appendix.

Chapter 3

Survey of Direction-parallel Milling

3.1 Introduction

3.1.1 Contents of the Chapter

We present a detailed description of a zigzag algorithm for $2\frac{1}{2}$D pocket machining. The algorithm is capable of computing the zigzag cutter path for any multiply-connected planar area ('pocket') bounded by a wide class of curves. Drilled holes and similar cavities can automatically be handled. The underlying geometric principles are simple enough for allowing the algorithm to be included in a CNC.

After discussing its fundamentals we put our emphasis on explaining the solution of some advanced geometrical and technological problems inherently connected with zigzag machining (e.g. an automatic determination of the optimal inclination of the zigzag lines). Based on our implementation of program packages for both, offset and zigzag milling we give a heuristic analysis and comparison of these machining strategies.

3.1.2 Problem Specification

In this chapter we restrict to techniques for zigzag (and zig[1]) milling. Similar to the previous chapter, we deal with the following problem:

Pocket Machining Problem (Zigzag/Zig Milling):

Given :

- boundary contours enclosing a multiply-connected planar area (a so-called 'pocket'),

- boundary contours of drilled holes and similar cavities,

- technological objectives and constraints.

Determine :

- a suitable cutter size,

- an optimal inclination of the cutter path,

- a correct (and with respect to some criteria hopefully optimal) cutter path for machining the pocket according to the technological requirements,

- predrill positions for tool plunges.

---

[1]Zig milling is derived from zigzag milling by replacing the sequence of left-to-right and right-to-left movements by a sequence of left-to-right (right-to-left, respectively) and air movements.

Contrary to the last chapter on offset curve milling, we do not explicitly restrict our algorithm to specific types of contour elements (such as straight lines and circular arcs). Rather, the presented scheme is powerful enough to deal with nearly any type of curve provided that a 'black box' for computing offset curves, intersections with lines, tangents, local extrema, and points of inflection is available.

Actually, for the sake of programming simplicity, up to now our own implementation ZIGPOCKET only supports contours consisting of straight line segments and circular arcs. Besides achieving computational simplicity this is justified by the fact that most of today's NC machines are only capable of executing linear and circular interpolations. But our scheme is completely prepared for handling general input data resulting from $2\frac{1}{2}$D machining of 3D objects possibly bounded by sculptured surfaces. Supposed that NC machines become more powerful in the near future, ZIGPOCKET can easily be adapted within its framework by simply exchanging or extending the service routines of the above cited 'black box'.

Nevertheless, we would like to remark that offsetting, for instance, becomes a rather difficult task if curves containing elements other than lines and circular arcs are involved[2]. Hence, a complex mathematical machinery may be required, cf. Klass [Kla83], Tiller and Hanson [TH84], Hoschek [Hos85], Saeed *et al* [S*88a], Farouki and Neff [FN89].

3.2 Motivation and Basic Aspects

Intuitively there is no significant difference between removing material by means of zigzag machining and colouring pixels by means of polygon filling, cf. Hégron [Heg88]. Hence, one might be tempted to compute and order the intersections of a horizontal line with the boundary. Obviously every odd interval could be output as a tool path segment. By incrementing the line's y-level (by a value depending on the requested tool overhang) and repeatedly applying this scheme, the pocket should be machined, cf. Bruckner [Bru82], Wang *et al* [W*87].

This simple scheme will work well for convex polygons; but it must not be applied to pockets of more complex shape due to the following reason: in the case that the horizontal line intersects the boundary in more than two points it would be necessary to lift the tool, move it in the air, and plunge it down for continuing the machining process (cf. Fig. 3.1).

---

[2]This increase in sophistication is due to the fact that intersection routines for handling more general elements such as cubic splines become more difficult and that these elements are not invariant under offsetting. For instance, the offset of a cubic spline is no longer a cubic spline.

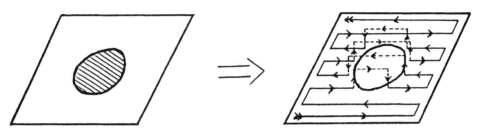

Figure 3.1: Complex Contours Cause Troubles.

But, in general, it is not possible to plunge down the tool onto the raw material without having a hole drilled previously. Most probably an additional production step is needed in order to have holes drilled before milling can take place. This undesirable production step clearly contributes to the total manufacturing expenses. Hence, tool retractions should be minimized.

Besides locally avoiding to move the tool in the air one should also reflect about some global strategy that would reduce à priori the number of tool retractions. Obviously, the total number of retractions depends on the geometry of the pocket and on the inclination of the zigzag path and on some additional factors to be investigated. For instance, for the sample contour depicted in Fig. 3.2, it is reasonable to incline the zigzag path by 90° since this permits to machine the pocket without necessarily moving in the air. In Section 3.5.1 we will present an algorithm that computes (near) optimum inclinations.

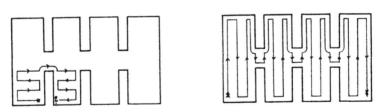

Figure 3.2: Different Inclinations of the Tool Path.

Up to now we have regarded contours as boundaries that must not be crossed by the tool. Indeed, normally a workpiece has to be put to the filings if the border contour or any other avoidance region ('positive' island) has been violated. But there do also exist contours that may (or even should) be crossed. These contours bound so-called 'negative' islands, i.e. regions of the pocket that have a surface lying below the actual machining level (e.g. holes and similar cavities).

As a matter of principle, one can distinguish between two main approaches to handling negative islands:

1. After shrinking the contour of the negative island for some amount (depending on the tool size) one can proceed as in the case of positive islands (i.e. during milling this region is spared).

2. During the computation of the zigzag path the negative islands are not excluded but during milling one uses rapid feed for passing over these regions. Of course, using rapid feed will save some amount of machining time (compared to using normal feed during 'machining' these regions).

Since it heavily depends on the geometry of the pocket and on the machining objectives which one of the two strategies is more convenient we have investigated the second approach, too.

The tool must not cut any material during rapid feed movements. Hence, for carrying out approach 2) it is not sufficient to simply compute the intersections of the zigzag segments with the boundaries of the negative islands and to drive the tool between corresponding intersections thereby using rapid feed. As depicted in Fig. 3.3, this strategy might cause several regions being damaged.

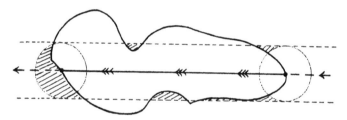

Figure 3.3: Using Rapid Feed.

3.3 Pocketing Features of ZIGPOCKET

Using methods and concepts of Computational Geometry we are able to give efficient solutions to the above stated major geometrical and technological problems of zigzag pocketing. In more detail, we have achieved the following outstanding features which make ZIGPOCKET a versatile tool for the practical machining of complicated mechanical parts.

3.3.1 Advanced Geometrical Features

- ZIGPOCKET is able to fully automatically compute the tool path for machining multiply-connected planar areas bounded by a wide class of curves.

Efficient machining is supported by its capability to use either **zigzag** or **zig**[3] machining.

- The powerful geometric concept of our method guarantees that the pocket is 'totally' milled, i.e. that any area which can be cut without violating the boundary will be cut. Furthermore, it is ensured that no contour is damaged no matter how complicated the shape of the pocket is. If requested, it is possible to leave different margins uncut at the border and island contours[4]. Thus, there is no need for a time-consuming and troublesome graphical verification of the tool path.

- ZigPocket executes some additional optimization tasks: As far as possible, retracting the tool is avoided and pocket areas are not machined repeatedly. Due to the first optimization criterion the number of predrill positions is minimized.

3.3.2   User Assistance and Advanced Technological Features

- ZigPocket proposes a (near) optimum inclination of the zigzag path.

- Drilled holes and similar cavities can automatically be handled. By using rapid feed above these regions the cutting time might be considerably reduced. In particular, this is of some importance if moulded workpieces have to be finished.

- Similar to GeoPocket, ZigPocket enables a computer-aided tool selection: With respect to a user-specified corner coverage parameter it determines an upper bound for the admissible size of the tool used for contour milling. Furthermore, depending on this selected value and on the minimal width at straits of the pocket contours a suitable size of the tool applied for zigzag milling is suggested. This feature has already been described in the previous chapter.

3.4   Solving Geometrical Problems of Pocketing

For this section, for the sake of simplicity we assume that the requested inclination is zero, i.e. that the segments of the zigzag path are parallel to the x-axis.

---

[3] True zigzag machining causes the tool to cut alternately with and against the spindle direction ('conventional' respectively 'climb' milling). Using zig milling it is possible to stick to either conventional or climb milling. This strategy usually ensures a better surface quality.

[4] This excess material is usually cleared away in the finishing step.

Furthermore, we restrict to pockets not containing negative islands. The handling of negative islands will be explained in the next section on technological problems of zigzag pocketing.

3.4.1 Constructing the Mesh

As illustrated in the previous section one has to be careful if the pocket area is not convex. We believe that it is reasonable to build up a data structure providing information on the global shape and connectivity of the pocket. This has been realized by constructing a 'mesh' consisting of the endpoints of the zigzag elements and local extrema of the boundary[5]. As a useful side-effect, performing this preprocessing step separates the computation of the endpoints of the zigzag elements from the actual construction of the tool path. The availability of this mesh will give us the possibility to perform some optimizations of the tool path thereby entirely working on the mesh.

In more detail (cf. Fig. 3.4), the 'mesh' is a graph-like structure where each node corresponds

- either to an endpoint of a zigzag path element, (i.e. to an intersection of a horizontal (zigzag) line with the outer border contour or with a positive island),

- or to a local minimum (maximum, respectively) of one of these contours with respect to y-coordinates.

Nodes of the first type are called 'original nodes' whereas those of the second type are called 'additional nodes'. Endpoints and extrema form the set of event points.

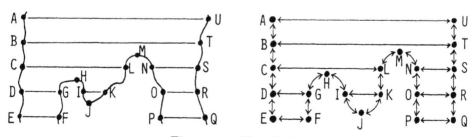

Figure 3.4: The Mesh.

---

[5]Obviously, the original boundary has to be offset by an offset equal to or larger than the radius of the tool used for zigzag machining. Otherwise, at the endpoints of the zigzag elements the tool would damage the borders of the pocket.

Define an edge to be 'horizontal' if it interconnects two nodes with equal y-coordinates. Otherwise, call it 'vertical'. Then, two nodes of the undirected graph are connected

- by a horizontal edge if both nodes are original nodes, or

- by a vertical edge if their corresponding contour points are located on the same contour and if it is possible to traverse this contour from one point to the second one thereby passing through no other points being nodes of the mesh.

It is easy to realize that every node has at most three incident edges, i.e. the graph is of degree three.

How can we obtain the mesh? This task is efficiently carried out by making use of the plane sweep paradigm, cf. Preparata and Shamos' book [PS88]. In order to help intuition, imagine that a horizontal line is 'sweeping' across the plane from bottom to top, reporting the sequence of intersection intervals of this line with the boundary, the so-called sweep-line status.

It is obvious that no change in the number of intervals will be found without sweeping over a local extremum (with respect to y-coordinates). Hence, only at event points the sweep-line status has to be modified. At an event corresponding to a local minimum (maximum, respectively), intervals of the sweep line have to be split up (have to be unified, respectively). In order to draw up the mesh it is sufficient to output the sweep-line status at events corresponding to original nodes. Additionally, appropriate vertical edges have to be established.

From a theoretical point of view, an interesting algorithm for computing the intersections of a line and a simple polygon, sorted in the order in which they occur along the line, has been published by Hoffmann *et al* [H*85]. By making use of finger search trees, an elegant linear-time solution can be obtained.

3.4.2 Computing the Tool Path

Suppose that the mesh is available. Then, constructing the zigzag path corresponds to finding a tour through the graph such that every horizontal edge has been traversed. Jumping between nodes not interconnected by edges (i.e. moving the tool in the air) is permitted but not recommended.

We have not tried to design an algorithm that attempts to solve something like a restricted traveling salesman problem[6] after having assigned a 'weight' or 'cost' to each edge. Instead, we have contented ourselves to guaranteeing that nothing is left uncut that could be cut without violating any contour.

---

[6]A path through a graph is called a traveling salesman tour if each node of the graph is visited exactly once and if the total length of the traversed edges is minimal, cf. [G*85].

Our goal is realized by stacking areas that cannot immediately be machined, cf. Fig. 3.5. Assume that the tool has been moved from left to right between two original nodes and is to move upwards. In this case, we proceed as follows in order to get from the actual y-level to the next higher level:

1. If the vertical edge incident upon the right node points to an original node then the tool is simply moved upwards along the contour to this new right node.

2. Otherwise, if the vertical edge incident upon the right node is pointing to an additional node we keep the tool moving in a right-upwards direction until an original node at the next (higher) level is found.

3. If the vertical edge incident upon the left node is pointing to an additional node we search in a left-upwards direction until an original node at the next (higher) level is found. Then the search is continued to the right until the left endnode of the horizontal edge incident upon the right endnode detected in 1) or 2) is found.

During the search in 2) and 3) intermediate original nodes – representing 'entry' nodes to not yet machined regions – are put on a stack. For the other three directions of movement this algorithm is executed with 'left/right' and 'upwards/downwards' properly exchanged.

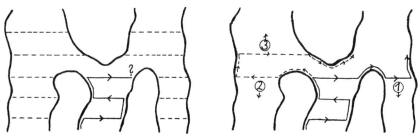

Figure 3.5: Stacking Not Yet Machined Regions.

Each time the tool has machined into a dead end, it has to be lifted and moved to a new pair of entry nodes popped from the stack. Actually, in our implementation this strict rule is weakened by performing some local optimization in order to get shorter moves. Flagging already visited nodes prevents machining a region twice.

Summarizing, constructing the zigzag path can be reduced to searching for a tour in the mesh. Although this approach could still be refined we believe that it should be sufficient for the practical application of ZIGPOCKET. We would like to remark that using the precomputed mesh enables us to guarantee that the pocket area is totally milled, no matter how complex its shape is.

3.5 Solving Technological Problems of Pocketing

Up to now we have only been concerned with solving the geometrical problems of zigzag machining. In this section we demonstrate how the important technological features of ZIGPOCKET have been realized.

3.5.1 Computing a (Near) Optimum Inclination

As it has been motivated by Fig. 3.2, it is reasonable to compute a suitable inclination of the zigzag path in order to reduce the number of tool retractions. In the following, we explain how ZIGPOCKET determines a (near) optimum inclination.

Recall the plane sweep paradigm used in Section 3.4.1 for constructing the mesh. When sweeping upwards each local minimum splits up the sweep line in two disjoint parts. Similarly, when moving downwards the sweep line is splitted by local maxima. Assume that the moving sweep line represents the tool moving on a zigzag path. In this case each extremum corresponds to a region that cannot be milled during the first pass. Hence, minimizing the number of local extrema (by selecting a suitable inclination) means minimizing the number of separated regions, i.e. the number of necessary movements in the air.

Our assumption only holds if 'the size of the tool is significantly smaller than the area to be machined'. This is due to the fact that the tool does not continuously sweep up and down but moves on zigzag lines at discrete y-levels. The smaller the tool is (relative to the size of the pocket), the smaller the distance is between the zigzag lines and the better our assumption of a continous sweep is fulfilled.

How can we compute an inclination such that the number of local extrema is minimized? This task is executed by analyzing 'reflex' profiles of contour elements. Before we can carry out our solution we have to make some terms more precise: A point shared by two consecutive contour elements is called a 'vertex'. A vertex is called 'reflex' if the internal angle between its incident elements is $> \pi$, 'tangential' if the angle equals π, and 'convex' otherwise. Similarly, assuming that the border contour[7] is counter-clockwise (CCW) oriented and that all island contours are clockwise (CW) oriented, an arc is said to be 'reflex' if it is CW oriented, 'convex' otherwise. A 'reflex' profile of contour elements is generated by picking out a reflex arc or reflex vertex and moving away in both directions (along the contour), until a convex vertex or convex arc is encountered.

Obviously, a particular set of suitable inclinations is associated with every reflex profile. If the profile makes an overall turn $< \pi$, the recommended angular area is depicted in Fig. 3.6. If the profile makes a turn equal to π this infinite set of recommended inclinations degenerates to one single value. Otherwise, no

---

[7]Additionally, all contour elements have to be subdivided at points of inflection. Obviously, this task is trivial in the case of lines and circular arcs.

inclination can be recommended – since one local extremum cannot be avoided – but there exists an angular area of forbidden inclinations which would yield two local extrema.

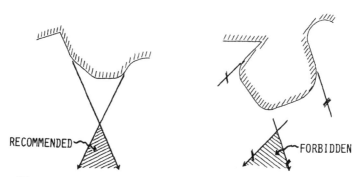

Figure 3.6: Recommended and Forbidden Inclinations.

Applying this method to all reflex profiles yields several intervals of recommended and forbidden inclinations. As a matter of principle, it seems to be hard to select a suitable inclination out of this infinite number. This task can be solved by using an algorithm similar to the computation of the measure of a union of intervals, cf. [PS88]. In general, the output of this algorithm will be a number of small intervals of inclinations all yielding the minimal number of local extrema, giving the possibility to impose some further selection criteria.

In strict mathematical terms this method does not always guarantee to find an inclination actually yielding the minimal number of retractions. Nevertheless, extensive field test have demonstrated that our method works satisfactorily. Results of this heuristic analysis are presented in Section 3.6.2.

3.5.2 Handling Negative Islands

Using rapid feed while the tool is cutting raw material may cause a bad surface quality. Even worse, using rapid feed while driving the tool into the raw material most probably results in a tool breakage. Hence, rapid feed may only be used while driving the tool over regions completely lying below the machining level[8]. Consequently, situations as depicted in Fig. 3.3 have to be avoided.

Assume that the tool is moving with rapid feed within the interior of a negative island. Roughly, avoiding to crash into the raw material can be achieved if care is taken that the center of the tool circle keeps out of a specific region near the contour of the negative island. This region is bounded by offsetting the

---

[8] As a matter of fact, scallop heights tend to be effectively greater than zero, i.e. machined surfaces are not totally smooth. Thus, when moving over already machined regions the tool is usually lifted by a small amount in order to avoid collision.

island contour by an offset $\rho + \epsilon(\rho)$, where ρ denotes the nominal radius of the tool. Usually, it is also requested that the tool should stop some amount $\epsilon(\rho)$ before the raw material is reached[9].

A crash can be algorithmically avoided by constructing the offset contour and restricting the usage of rapid feed. But this method still is not optimal. On one hand, it is too weak because the tool circle should have left the raw material at least with its front half before a rapid feed move can be started. Thus, in order to get a satisfying surface quality, each time when leaving the raw material the tool has to be driven for some additional amount of length.

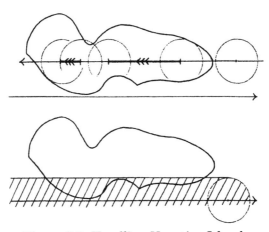

Figure 3.7: Handling Negative Islands.

On the other hand, the method is too restrictive if the tool has already been driven along a zigzag segment lying immediately below or above the actual segment. In this case, one has to take into account that some portion – the width is depending on the tool overhang – of the raw material covered when moving along the actual segment has already been cut. By modifying the method as depicted in Fig. 3.7 we are able to handle this case.

This general method for handling negative islands has been implemented in ZIGPOCKET. Although the principal idea is rather simple, the algorithm needs a careful implementation in order to ensure correct working even in exceptional cases.

3.5.3 Avoiding to Drill Unnecessary Holes

By means of selecting a suitable inclination we will most probably have achieved a considerable reduction of the number of different areas which have to be milled

---

[9]This security distance depends on the size of the tool. Normally, $\epsilon(\rho)$ equals about 20% of the tool radius ρ.

separately. Nevertheless, as a matter of fact, any minimization of this number is only possible within the limitations imposed by the geometry of the pocket. Hence, in the case of a very complex-shaped pocket one has to expect that it will not be possible to execute zigzag machining in one single pass, without retracting the tool.

In this case holes would have to be predrilled. Can this task be avoided? Indeed, this is possible if a small increase of the total path length is acceptable. The key to success is to ensure that any region to be machined is entered from an already machined region. In this case, the tool can be plunged onto this region and moved to the uncut area, cf. Fig. 3.8. It is easy to understand that by means of our stacking mechanism the unmachined regions are kept in proper order for executing this approach.

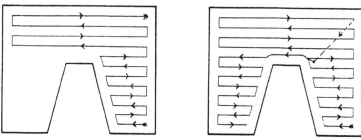

Figure 3.8: Avoiding to Drill Holes.

Clearly, sticking to the fixed order of the stack makes it nearly impossible to perform a global optimization in order to achieve short moves in the air. A similar contradiction may also arise with respect to a number of other optimization criteria ZIGPOCKET tries to fulfill. These contradictions cannot be solved by the package but it is the sole responsibility of the user to carefully consider the pros and cons and to select the suitable combination of ZIGPOCKET's features.

3.6 Practical Results and Heuristic Analysis

3.6.1 The Program Package GEOPOCKET/ZIGPOCKET

Our program package GEOPOCKET/ZIGPOCKET emerged out of diverse work on designing algorithms for pocket machining, starting in the beginning of 1986. The first algorithms have been implemented about one year later. Since this time, we have gradually extended our package up to its current functionality.

GEOPOCKET/ZIGPOCKET have been written in ANSI FORTRAN 77. On one hand, coding the algorithms in FORTRAN ensured the portability of our package and its applicability in industry. On the other hand, it took us a lot of troubles in order to implement recursion and realize advanced data structures. Anyway, the actual implementation of our algorithms provided us with the possibility to carry out a comprehensive heuristic analysis presented in the following paragraphs.

3.6.2   How Important Is a Suitable Inclination?

Wang *et al* [W*87] have analyzed the relationship between the length of the zigzag path and the selected inclination. Restricting to simple polygons (triangles to heptagons), they have observed that, as a heuristic rule-of-thumb, the zigzag path should be inclined such that it is parallel to the longest edge of the polygon.

We have designed several programs for producing input data for testing. As a matter of principle, we can confirm the above stated result of [W*87]. In more detail, we can quote our observations as follows:

- For simple polygons (such as triangles, rectangles, pentagons, etc.), there seems to exist a significant correlation between the length and the selected inclination of the zigzag tool path[10].

- This correlation becomes rather apparent for medium-sized[11] tools whereas this effect gradually diminishes with decreasing/increasing size. For large tools it is merely a matter of chance than of any clear rule whether the tool path is long or short for a specific inclination.

- For medium-sized tools, the average variation seems to lie in the range of 4–8 percent. The difference between the best and the worst case is of the order of 10–15 percent of the total length. For small tools, this percentage goes to zero because the total length of the path is increasing much faster than the difference between the longest and shortest path.

- The simple rule-of-thumb does not hold for complex pockets possibly containing some positive islands. Similarly, the correspondence between inclination and path length becomes less significant with increasing number of contour elements, even if the overall shape of the pocket is not varied. For pockets bounded by a lot of arcs it seems to be nearly impossible to predict a reasonable inclination (in order to get minimal tool path length).

- Whereas the impact of the inclination on the resulting length decreases with increasing complexity of the pocket, a strong relationship between the inclination and the number of separate regions (i.e. tool retractions) can be observed. As expected, selecting a suitable inclination becomes the

---

[10] In our analysis, a zigzag tool path consists of the actual zigzag path and of the path used for driving the tool along the contour for one time.

[11] We call a tool 'medium-sized' if an NC programmer normally would use a tool of about this size. Clearly, all sizes have to be defined relative to the 'size' of the pocket to be machined.

more important, the smaller the tool and the more complex the shape of the pocket are.

- Our approach to compute an optimal inclination does not guarantee to achieve a mimimal number of retractions. Nevertheless, for medium-sized (or small-sized) tools a near optimum usually is found, at least. This is of particular importance in the case of complex-shaped pockets where for a human, too, it is difficult to propose a reasonable inclination.

Summarizing, for simple-shaped pockets it seems to be reasonable to select an inclination parallel to one of the longest edges of the input contour. In the case of a more complex shape, our algorithm for selecting an inclination is applicable, producing (near) optimum results.

3.6.3   Zigzag Versus Offset Curve Milling

In short terms, there seems to be no significant correlation between the tool path lengths of both milling strategies. For medium-sized tools, the length of a tool path generated by offset curve milling will range about in the top quarter of the zigzag lengths, sometimes being even a little bit shorter. The larger the tool and the more complicated the shape of the pocket area, the better offset curve milling seems to be. For rather simple shapes or when utilizing a small tool it seems to be more advantageous to use zigzag milling.

3.7   Concluding Remarks

3.7.1   Summary

In the previous sections we have presented an overall description of our pocketing package ZIGPOCKET. Summarizing, we can state its main features as follows: The package is able to handle any multiply-connected pocket area bounded by a wide class of curves. It is possible to deal with positive as well as negative islands. Solving a lot of technological problems, our approach meets most practical requirements of the shop floor.

We have achieved extremely fast computations. For instance, on a VAXstation 2000 running VMS, the CPU-consumption of about 200 tested contour files has always been in the range of 1 to 10 seconds. For most practical applications the CPU-time will be considerably less than 5 seconds. For sample examples, we refer to the appendix.

There is no need for verifying the tool path. Hence, included into a CNC, ZIGPOCKET seems to be a valuable tool for preparing correct geometrical and technological data for the 'total' milling of multiply-connected pockets within reasonably short CPU-time.

3.7.2 Open Problems

Although ZigPocket is a sophisticated package, it could still be refined. For instance, it would be desirable to handle 'half-open' pockets, i.e. areas that are not bounded by closed contours. Obviously, half-open pockets can easily be simulated by closed pockets. However, this extension is of some importance for practical applications because it enables additional optimizations of the tool path, which cannot be realized when dealing with closed contours.

Our work has revealed two issues for theoretical research: Our approach to computing a suitable inclination performs satisfactorily in industrial applications of ZigPocket although it is not guaranteed that an inclination yielding the minimal number of retractions is found. Seen from a theoretical point of view, it would be interesting to design an algorithm that can be proved to solve the requested problem (and not just a very similar one). More generally, it might be interesting to investigate whether an algorithm for computing a traveling salesman tour for our specific mesh can be executed within a polynomial[12] amount of time.

---

[12] As a matter of fact, the general decision problem for traveling salesman tours is known to be $\mathcal{NP}$-complete, cf. Grötschel *et al* [G*85].

Chapter 4

Preliminaries

This chapter surveys the background material used within the book. Besides stating notational conventions, we summarize basic concepts of topology, geometry, graph theory, and algorithm theory. We expect the reader to be familiar with these basic concepts. Hence, except for the first section, we do not recommend to go thoroughly through all the definitions. They have mainly been included for reference.

4.1   Notational Conventions

Before continuing, we offer a collection of names and typed variables that appear throughout this book. Adopting the notation scheme presented in Edelsbrunner's textbook [Ede87], the names used for the various objects in this book can be categorized in the following list:

- upper case blackboard bold,

- upper case script,

- upper case roman,

- lower case roman,

- lower case greek.

Below, each category is dealt with in more detail. For each category, the common properties are briefly described and a list of names used and of objects named in this way is stated.

4.1.1   Upper Case Blackboard Bold

We denote the basic data types of calculus by upper case blackboard bold font. The basic data types used are

$\mathbb{B}$	which represents boolean (i.e. true and false),
$\mathbb{E}$	which represents the Euclidean space (i.e. $\mathbb{R}$ under the topology imposed by the Euclidean distance measure),
$\mathbb{N}$	which represents the natural numbers,
$\mathbb{N}_0$	which represents the natural numbers with zero added,
$\mathbb{R}$	which represents the reals.

4.1.2 Upper Case Script

Upper case script is used for objects bearing a structure that is more complicated than the structure of a set. Typical examples are provided by regions, contours, and graphs.

$\mathcal{A}$	(planar) area,
$\mathcal{B}$	boundary,
$\mathcal{C}$	contour,
$\mathcal{G}$	graph,
$\mathcal{M}$	mesh (of the zigzag path),
$\mathcal{MA}$	machinable area,
$\mathcal{N}$	contour of a negative island,
$\mathcal{P}$	pocket,
$\mathcal{TP}$	tool path,
$\mathcal{TS}$	area defined by the tool swept,
$\mathcal{VA}$	Voronoi area,
$\mathcal{VD}$	Voronoi diagram,
$\mathcal{VP}$	Voronoi polygon,
$\mathcal{VR}$	Voronoi region,
$\mathcal{ZL}$	arrangement of zigzag lines,
$\mathcal{ZS}$	arrangement of zigzag line segments.

4.1.3 Upper Case Roman

Upper case roman is used for sets and similar collections bearing little or no structure.

B	set of bisectors,
C	curve or circle,
D	disk,
E	set of edges (of a graph),
I	interval,
N	set of nodes (of a graph),
O	set of objects or Offset set,
P	set of points or path (in a graph),
S	set of segments,
T	tree or tour in a graph,
V	set of vertices (of a contour).

Subset relations are denoted by $\subset$ and $\subseteq$, where $\subset$ denotes a strict subset relation (excluding equality). Similarly, supersets are denoted by $\supset$ and $\supseteq$.

4.1.4 Lower Case Roman

Lower case roman letters are widely used throughout this book. Normally, they denote simple objects such as points, lines, etc. We have tried to stick as tightly as possible to the following rules. Nevertheless, we are aware that some of the following symbols have been 'abused' in a specific context.

b	bisector,
c	center (of a circle) or circular arc,
d	Euclidean distance,
e	edge,
f	parameterization of a curve,
i	index,
j	auxiliary for index,
k	number of reflex vertices,
l	auxiliary for index,
ℓ	line (segment),
m	number of island contours,
n	number of contour objects/segments,
o	object,
p	point,
q	auxiliary for point,
r	ray,
s	segment,
t	tangent line/vector or contour offset,
v	vertex or node,
w	width of a strait,
x	x-coordinate,
y	y-coordinate,
z	z-coordinate.

Usually all points lie in E^2.

4.1.5 Lower Case Greek

Lower case greek letters are normally used for denoting real values such as angles, parameters, etc.

α	real number,
β	real number,
γ	real number,

δ	real number (distance),
ϵ	real number (usually small and positive),
θ	angle,
λ	scaling factor,
ρ	radius of a circle,
ϕ	angle,
ψ	angle.

Besides, π is used for denoting 180 degrees in radians.

4.2 Topology and Geometry Revisited

For a point $p = (x, y) \in \mathbb{R}^2$, the l_2- or *Euclidean norm* is given by $\|p\| := \sqrt{x^2 + y^2}$. This norm induces the *Euclidean distance* $d(p, q) := \|p - q\|$ between two points p and q. For two sets $P, Q, d(P, Q) := \inf \{d(p, q) : p \in P \text{ and } q \in Q\}$; i.e. the Euclidean distance of two sets is the largest lower bound on Euclidean distances of their members. The distance $d(p, Q)$ is commonly referred to as the *offset* or *clearance* distance of p with respect to the set Q.

For any positive real number ρ, the set $D(c, \rho) := \{p : d(p, c) < \rho\}$ is the *open disk* with center c and radius ρ. Similarly, $C(c, \rho)$ denotes the set $\{p : d(p, c) = \rho\}$, i.e. the *circle* with center c and radius ρ.

A set P is *bounded* if there exists an open disk that contains P, and P is *unbounded*, otherwise. A set P is *open* if, for every $p \in P$, there exists an open disk centered at p that is completely contained in P. P is *closed* if its complement $\complement P$ is open. The *interior* $\underline{P}$ of P is the largest open subset of P, and the *closure* $\overline{P}$ of P is the smallest closed set containing P. The *boundary* ∂P is given by $\overline{P} \setminus \underline{P}$, i.e. the set of points in $\overline{P}$ not contained in $\underline{P}$.

Given two disjoint points p and q, the *open straight line segment* (p, q) through p, q is given by the set $\{(1 - \lambda)p + \lambda q : \lambda \in (0..1)\}$. Similarly, the *closed straight line segment* $\overline{(p, q)}$ through p, q is given by the set $\{(1 - \lambda)p + \lambda q : \lambda \in [0..1]\}$. The *line* $\ell(p, q)$ through p, q is given by $\{(1 - \lambda)p + \lambda q : \lambda \in \mathbb{R}\}$. The *ray* $r(p, q)$ originating at p and extending through q to infinity is given by $\{(1 - \lambda)p + \lambda q : \lambda \in \mathbb{R}_0^+\}$.

More generally, a triple (C, f, I) is a *curve* if f is a mapping $f : I \subset \mathbb{E} \mapsto \mathbb{E}^2$ such that $f(I) = C$ and f is continuous and partially continuously differentiable. The mapping f is called a *parameterization* of C. The single coordinate functions of f are denoted by f_x and f_y. For instance, a circular arc with center c and radius ρ is parameterized by $f_x(\phi) := c_x + \rho \cos \phi$ and $f_y := c_y + \rho \sin \phi$. For short-hand, we often will omit f and I if we are only interested in the set C. Observe that f imposes an orientation on the curve. It is convenient to define the open curve $\underline{C}$ as the curve C with endpoints omitted. Similarly, $\overline{C}$ and ∂C are defined.

The curve (C, f, I), with $I = [\alpha..\beta]$, is *closed*[1] if $f(\alpha) = f(\beta)$. The curve is *simple* if $f(\gamma_1) \neq f(\gamma_2)$ for any $\gamma_1 \neq \gamma_2 \in (\alpha..\beta)$. A simple and closed curve is called a *Jordan curve*. By the *Jordan curve theorem*, a Jordan curve C partitions E^2 into two disjoint regions, the *interior* (bounded) and the *exterior* (unbounded) that are separated by C.

The set of points on one side of a line is called an *(open) half-space*. A *closed half-space* is the union of an open half-space and its boundary.

A set P is *convex* if, for any two points $p, q \in P$, the line segment $\overline{(p, q)}$ is entirely contained in P. A set P is *star-shaped* if there exists a point $p \in P$ such that for all points $q \in P$ the line segment $\overline{(p, q)}$ lies entirely in P. The locus of points p having this property is called the *kernel* of P. A set P is called *generalized-star-shaped* with *nucleus* $N \subset P$ if for all points $q \in P$ there exists a point $p \in N$ such that the line segment $\overline{(p, q)}$ lies entirely in P.

A set P is *connected* if it cannot be partitioned into two disjoint, open (in the relative topology) subsets P_1, P_2 such that $P = P_1 \cup P_2$. The connected components of P are the maximal connected subsets of P. A set P is *simply-connected* if each connected component of $\complement P$ is unbounded, *multiply-connected* otherwise. Two points $p, q \in P$ are *path-connected* if there exists a curve entirely contained in P, starting in p and ending in q (i.e. $f(\alpha) = p$ and $f(\beta) = q$). A set P is *path-connected* if every pair of points $p, q \in P$ is path-connected. We would like to remark that, under the Euclidean topology, for any open set P being 'connected' is equivalent to being 'path-connected'. Furthermore, P is simply-connected iff[2] any closed curve lying entirely in P can continuously be shrinked to a point without leaving P.

4.3 Graph Theory Revisited

A *graph* $\mathcal{G} = (N, E)$ consists of a finite set N of nodes and a finite set E of edges, i.e. pairs of nodes. If every edge is an unordered pair $\{u, v\}$ of nodes then $\mathcal{G}$ is an *undirected* graph. $\mathcal{G}$ is a *directed* graph – a so-called *digraph* – if every edge is an order pair (u, v) of nodes. In both cases, the nodes u, v associated with an edge e are called its *endnodes* and e is *incident* upon u and v. The nodes u and v connected by e are said to be *adjacent* to each other. A graph is *complete* if it contains all possible pairs of nodes as edges.

In the case of a digraph, u is called the *initial endnode* (or *tail* or *origin*), and v is called the *terminal endnode* (or *head* or *destination*). Hence, e is an *outgoing edge* of u and an *incoming edge* of v. The cardinality of the set of incoming (outgoing) edges is called the *indegree* (*outdegree*, respectively). The sum of the

---

[1] We are aware of the name-clash arising from this second definition of 'closed'. However, it should become clear by the context which meaning of 'closed' is intended.

[2] As usual, 'iff' stands for 'if and only if'.

indegree and the outdegree yields the total number of incident edges, called the *degree* of the node.

A sequence $P = (v_1, \ldots, v_n)$ of nodes is a *path* in a (directed) graph if each pair $\{v_i, v_{i+1}\}$ ((v_i, v_{i+1}), respectively) is an edge of $\mathcal{G}$. An undirected graph $\mathcal{G}$ is *connected* if every two nodes of $\mathcal{G}$ can be connected by a path. A digraph is *strongly connected* if there is a path between every two nodes of $\mathcal{G}$; a digraph is *weakly connected* if $\mathcal{G}$ regarded as an undirected graph is connected.

A *(rooted) tree* is a directed graph $\mathcal{T} = (N, E)$ that is weakly connected and where each node is the head of exactly one edge, except for one node that is called the *root* of $\mathcal{T}$. By convention, the heads of outgoing edges are called *sons* of their origin, the so-called *father*. A node v is called a successor of u if v is a son of u or v is a successor of a son of u. *Leafs* are those nodes that have no sons. The *height* of $\mathcal{G}$ is the maximal number of nodes of paths in $\mathcal{T}$ (originating at the root). A *spanning tree* of a graph $\mathcal{G}$ is a tree containing all nodes of $\mathcal{G}$, and whose edges are edges of $\mathcal{G}$.

A graph is a *weighted graph* if a real number – the so-called *weight* or *cost* – is associated with each edge. The weight of a graph is commonly regarded as the sum of the weights of its edges. Spanning trees with minimal weight are called *minimal spanning trees* (MST). In the case of the weight denoting the Euclidean distance between (points associated with) the nodes, the minimal spanning tree is called *Euclidean minimal spanning tree* (EMST). A path visiting each node of a (complete) graph exactly once is called a *traveling salesman tour* (TST) if its weight is minimal.

A graph is *planar* if there exists a planar embedding of its edges such that no pair of edges intersect (except in their endpoints). For a planar graph, the number of edges $|E|$ is related to the number of nodes $|N|$ and the number of disjoint faces $|F|$ by Euler's Formula $|V| - |E| + |F| = 2$, cf. the textbook of Mäntylä [Man88].

4.4 Remarks on Algorithms

Algorithms are described in a high-level language similar to PASCAL or MODULA-2. Our notation will stick to their rigorous control structure, cf. Wirth's introduction [Wir88] to MODULA-2. However, we will be rather flexible concerning the 'syntax' of other statements. In particular, we will freely mix conventional mathematical notations with natural language expressions.

Names of procedures are stated in sans serif style. The control structures are written in **bold face**. For indicating the type of a parameter passed to a procedure, we have adopted the following notation:

- A downwards arrow $\downarrow$ indicates an input parameter (whose value is not changed within the procedure).

- An upwards arrow ↑ indicates an output parameter.

- An upwards-downwards arrow ↕ indicates a transient parameter (i.e. a parameter that conveys a value into the procedure and receives a new value there).

When carrying out a proof, we find it convenient to use some common abbreviations. For shorthand, we write

- *w.r.t.* instead of 'with respect to',

- *s.t.* instead of 'such that',

- *w.l.o.g.* instead of 'without loss of generality'.

In order to state the time complexities of our algorithms we use a notational scheme popularized by Knuth [Knu76]. In the following, let the involved functions f, g be defined over $\mathbb{N}$. Then,

$$O(f) \quad := \quad \{g : (\exists \alpha > 0, n_o) \text{ s.t. } (\forall n \geq n_0) \, g(n) \leq \alpha f(n)\},$$
$$\Omega(f) \quad := \quad \{g : (\exists \alpha > 0, n_o) \text{ s.t. } (\forall n \geq n_0) \, g(n) \geq \alpha f(n)\},$$
$$\Theta(f) \quad := \quad O(f) \cap \Omega(f).$$

Furthermore, g is *constant* if $g \in O(1)$, *logarithmic* if $g \in O(\log n)$, *linear* if $g \in O(n)$, and *quadratic* if $g \in O(n^2)$.

Obviously, all these terms express the asymptotic behaviour of g. Hence, if n denotes the size of the input and $g(n)$, with $g \in O(f)$, denotes the number of steps the algorithm requires for performing its calculation, then $g(n)$ resembles $f(n)$ the better the larger n is. It is therefore quite possible that an $O(n^2)$-algorithm, for instance, outperforms an $O(n \log n)$ algorithm for any input size n appearing in practice.

In addition, when speaking about the time complexity of an algorithm it would be better to deal with the average-case complexity instead of the worst-case complexity. However, a mathematical average-case analysis usually is much more complicated than the worst-case analysis. Furthermore, it may be difficult to select a distribution that constitutes a realistic model for practice.

Due to this reason, we have also contented ourselves to mathematically analyzing the worst-case complexity. Additionally, heuristics are stated concerning the average or 'practical' case.

Classical books on algorithm theory have been published by Knuth [Knu68], [Knu69], [Knu73] and Aho *et al* [A*74]. For up-to-date introductions we refer to the books of Mehlhorn [Meh84a], [Meh84b], [Meh84c], Wirth [Wir86], Baase [Baa88], and Sedgewick [Sed88].

Part II

Contour-parallel Milling

Chapter 5

Computing Voronoi Diagrams

5.1 Introduction

5.1.1 Previous and Related Work on Voronoi Diagrams

Voronoi diagrams of points in the plane have been first introduced by the emigré Russian mathematician Voronoi in his treatise [Vor08] on the geometry of numbers. Voronoi diagrams have been reinvented and studied by researchers in several fields. They have been applied in geology, geography, meteorology, and crystallography. In the mathematical sciences, Voronoi diagrams have been used for simulating differential equations by finite element methods and for interpolating surfaces in geometric modeling systems. Euclidean minimum spanning trees as well as largest empty circles can be computed by means of Voronoi diagrams, too. For an extensive list of references for diverse applications, we refer to Avis and Bhattacharya [AB83]. More recent surveys on Voronoi diagrams have been published by Aurenhammer [Aur88] and by Klein [Kle89]. In some works, the alternative terminology 'Thiessen' or 'Dirichlet' tesselation is used instead of the term Voronoi diagram. This terminology dates back to Thiessen's work [Thi11] and Dirichlet's investigation [Dir50].

The Voronoi diagram of a set P of points in the plane is a partition of the plane such that each region of the partition represents the locus of points that are closer (under the Euclidean metric) to one member of P than to any other member. This definition contains four items – set of points, plane, Euclidean metric, one member – which are susceptible of generalization.

Indeed, during the last years many generalizations and variations of Voronoi diagrams have been studied. However, most works are only dealing with sets of points. Very few successful approaches to handling Voronoi diagrams of general objects in more than two dimensions are known. Most of the research in this area is motivated by path planning problems arising from robotics. Reference is given to Canny's 'roadmaps' published in his Ph.D. thesis [Can87,CD88], and to the axiomatic approach of Stifter generalizing Voronoi diagrams and the retraction method to three dimensions. In her Ph.D. thesis [Sti88], the definition of Voronoi diagrams is not restricted to a specific class of objects. Rather, a general set of axioms is set up and all objects satisfying these axioms can be handled. Nevertheless, the problem of algorithmically handling Voronoi diagrams of complex objects in three or more dimensions is still open for future research.

Returning to two dimensions, Blum's concept of 'medial axis' has to be noted, cf. [Blu67,Blu74]. Originating from biological applications, it constitutes a means to describe a polygonal figure. Lateron, a number of papers have been published on the Voronoi diagram of a simple polygon; see for instance Preparata's publication [Pre77]. Alternate terminologies for the Voronoi diagram restricted to the interior of a simple polygon include the term 'internal skeleton'.

Most of the early papers on Voronoi diagrams – no matter whether defined by a set of points or by a set of line segments – rely on an incremental construction of the diagram. This means that the diagram is iteratively constructed, obtaining the 'new' diagram defined by a set of $k + 1$ elements by means of insertion of the new element and 'local' update of the 'old' diagram defined by a set of k elements. Unfortunately, applied to a set of n elements these approaches exhibit an $O(n^2)$ worst-case (and even average-case) time behaviour because the necessary updates may be not as local as it would be desirable in order to achieve a better complexity bound.

With the advent of computational geometry, a number of more efficient algorithms have been proposed. In the following list we give a survey on recent approaches that are asymptotically efficient:

- The first $O(n \log n)$ algorithm for computing the Voronoi diagram of a set of n points in the plane has been published by Shamos and Hoey in [SH75]. Since any Voronoi algorithm is required to take $O(n \log n)$ time in the worst case[1], the algorithm is worst-case optimal. Their algorithm uses the divide-and-conquer paradigm. The key observation is that the Voronoi diagram of a set P can be obtained by suitably partitioning P into two disjoint subsets P_L and P_R of equal size and by 'merging' the (recursively) computed subdiagrams. The actual heart of this algorithm, the so-called Shamos-Hoey scan for merging two subdiagrams, runs in linear time. This scheme has been presented in detail in Lee's report [Lee78] on proximity and reachability. A couple of improvements of the Shamos-Hoey algorithm, in particular with respect to implementational issues, have been published in Horspool's report [Hor79].

- The problem of computing the Voronoi diagram of a set of disjoint polygonal and circular objects has been first studied by Drysdale in his Ph.D. thesis [Dry79]. He achieved a subquadratic solution. Subsequently, Lee and Drysdale improved the algorithm obtaining an $O(n \log^2 n)$ upper bound, cf. [LD81].

- Dealing with a collection of disjoint points and open line segments, Kirkpatrick proposed an $O(n \log n)$ divide-and-conquer algorithm in his conference paper [Kir79]. His ideas of imposing 'spokes' on the Voronoi diagram under construction and using an Euclidean minimum spanning tree for

---

[1]This lower bound on the worst-case complexity can be established by means of a linear-time transformation to sorting, which is known to take $\Omega(n \log n)$ time in the algebraic computation-tree model, cf. [PS88]. Roughly, the Voronoi diagram of a set of points in one dimension consists of a sorted sequence of bisectors separating adjacent points. Hence, any algorithm for computing Voronoi diagrams is able to sort.

initializing the merge procedure are of great interest. Unfortunately, the overall algorithm is rather complicated.

- Improving Preparata's algorithm [Pre77], Lee published an $O(n \log n)$ divide-and-conquer algorithm for computing the medial axis of a simple polygon, cf. [Lee82].

- In [Sha85], Sharir proposed an $O(n \log^2 n)$ algorithm for computing the Voronoi diagram of a collection of circles that may intersect arbitrarily.

- Subsuming the earlier work on constructing Voronoi diagrams for a set of disjoint line segments and circular arcs, Yap came up with a sophisticated worst-case optimal algorithm, cf. [Yap85,Yap87].

Common to all of the above cited asymptotically efficient algorithms is the fact that they make use of the divide-and-conquer paradigm. Recently, Fortune outlined an elegant technique for obtaining the Voronoi diagram of line segment sites in worst-case optimal time, cf. [For85,For86,For87b]. Its main idea is to recover the diagram by executing a plane-sweep technique in a transformation space. Unfortunately, to our knowledge no details of implementations of Fortune's and Yap's algorithm have been published.

In [O*84], Ohya *et al* polished the incremental construction scheme for the Voronoi diagram of a set of points. In the worst case, their algorithm still suffers from a quadratic time behaviour but they succeeded in proving a linear average-case complexity. Their approach has been further refined by Sugihara and Iri, cf. [SI89a,SI89b].

5.1.2   Our Approach to Constructing Voronoi Diagrams

In the sequel we present a detailed description of our approach to constructing Voronoi diagrams. Our approach is mainly motivated by the following heuristic facts and requirements arising from the pocketing practice:

1. Pocket contours tend to exhibit a lot of geometric degeneracies such as parallel lines, concentric arcs, co-horizontal and co-vertical endpoints, symmetries, etc. Thus, 'general positions' must not be assumed.

2. Normally, a pocket contains no or only a rather small number of islands. Hence, our Voronoi algorithm should be well-suited for simply-connected pockets. In particular, NC programmers expect that pockets of simple shape are efficiently processed without computational overhead.

3. If a pocket contains a lot of islands then the individual islands usually are rather simply-shaped such as circular discs or rectangles.

4. Anyway, the computation of the Voronoi diagram can be started as soon as the input geometry has been fixed. Thus, computing Voronoi diagrams can be regarded as a preprocessing step.

Due to items 1, 2 and 3, for simply-connected pockets we decided to extend Lee's algorithm to straight line segments and circular arcs. In the case of multiply-connected pockets, we construct the individual Voronoi diagram for each contour and obtain the final Voronoi diagram by iteratively merging these single diagrams together. It turns out that the necessary merge procedure, i.e. the actual heart of our incremental process, is nearly identical to the merge procedure used for obtaining the diagram of a simply-connected contour by means of our adaption of Lee's divide-and-conquer algorithm. Hence, besides a program for computing these single diagrams, nearly no additional code is necessary for computing the final diagram of a multiply-connected area.

The advantage of this simple scheme with respect to more sophisticated approaches – such as [Kir79], [For86], [Yap87] – is that no restricting assumptions are necessary and that the provided information on the contours is exploited whereas Yap and Fortune have to struggle with more general settings. Applying one of these two approaches, there seems to be no possibility to gain some speed-up when dealing with elements grouped within closed curves instead of being arbitrarily scattered in the plane. Hence, when dealing with a simply-connected pocket one may expect that a Voronoi algorithm based on Lee's approach is faster than an algorithm based on Yap's or Fortune's ideas. Unfortunately, we could not manage to get a VAX/VMS implementation of one of these algorithms in order to be able to compare the CPU-time consumptions.

From a complexity point of view, the drawback of our approach is constituted by its worst-case behaviour. For a pocket bounded by one outer boundary contour and m island contours, the algorithm can take up to $O(n \cdot m + n \log n)$ time where n stands for the overall number of contour elements. This bound is (nearly) optimal for $m \ll n$. Clearly, if $m \approx n$ then our approach may exhibit an $O(n^2)$ time behaviour. Anyway, practical applications have not yet confirmed this theoretical disadvantage.

Our Voronoi algorithm has been designed and implemented in the years 1986 and 1987, cf. [Hel87b,Hel87a]. Recently, we have been informed by Srinivasan that a very similar approach – restricted to domains bounded by simple polygons – has been persued at IBM Yorktown Heights. Results have been published by Srinivasan and Nackman in [SN87]. In the companion paper [MS87], an interesting application of Voronoi diagrams to the computation of equivalent resistance networks in the fields of VLSI design is presented. These papers led to a minor simplification of our algorithm.

After Persson's initial suggestion in 1978, our work seems to constitute the first application of the concept of Voronoi diagrams to the pocket machining

problem. In particular, we are the first to present a thorough study of offsetting
by means of Voronoi diagrams.

5.2   Basic Concepts

5.2.1   Restrictions Imposed on the Pocket Contours

Definition 5.1 A *(contour) segment s* is either an open straight line segment
or an open circular arc (not greater than a semi-circle), with the 'standard'
parameterization associated. Points and segments are called *objects*.

Note that a segment cannot degenerate to a single point because it has to be
an open curve.

Definition 5.2 A set O of objects is called *complete* if

1. for every segment $s \in O$, its endpoints are in O,

2. for every point $p \in O$, there exists $s \in O$ s.t. p is an endpoint of s,

3. all objects of O are pairwise disjoint.

Points of a complete set of objects are called *vertices*. When dealing with sets
of objects, we usually presuppose that they are complete. These definitions serve
for defining the class of contours we will deal with.

Definition 5.3 (Pocket Contours) Let $\mathcal{P}$ be a multiply-connected, planar,
open area (a so-called pocket). $\mathcal{P}$ is called *admissible* if there exists a collection
$\mathcal{B}(\mathcal{P})$ of Jordan curves $\mathcal{C}_0, \ldots, \mathcal{C}_m$ s.t.

1. $\mathcal{B}(\mathcal{P}) = \partial\overline{\mathcal{P}}$,

2. $\mathcal{P}$ is the area in the interior of $\mathcal{C}_0$ and in the exterior of $\mathcal{C}_i$ (for all $1 \le i \le m$),

3. for all $0 \le i \ne j \le m$, $\mathcal{C}_i \cap \mathcal{C}_j = \emptyset$,

4. for all $0 \le i \le m$, $\mathcal{C}_i$ is a complete set of objects[2].

Boundaries $\mathcal{B}(\mathcal{P})$ meeting these conditions are called *proper*.

In the following, we restrict to admissible pockets bounded by proper bound-
ary curves. For simplicity, we often write $\mathcal{B}$ instead of $\mathcal{B}(\mathcal{P})$. The outmost curve
$\mathcal{C}_0$ is called the *border contour*. The inner curves $\mathcal{C}_1, \ldots, \mathcal{C}_m$ are called the *island
contours*. Throughout the book, we assume that the border contour is parame-
terized counter-clockwise (CCW) whereas the island contours are parameterized
clockwise (CW). Hence, the pocket area $\mathcal{P}$ lies on the left side of each contour.
When dealing with a normal vector, we will assume that it points inwards.

---

[2]In strict mathematical terms, we would have to distinguish between $\mathcal{C}$ being a set of objects
and $\mathcal{C}$ being an infinite set of points (i.e. a curve).

Definition 5.4 A vertex v is called *reflex* if the internal angle between the segments incident upon v is $> \pi$, *tangential* if the internal angle is equal to π, and *convex* otherwise. A circular arc is called *reflex* if it is a CW arc, and *convex* otherwise.

Fig. 5.1 illustrates this definition. By convention, n denotes the total number of segments and k stands for the total number of reflex vertices. Trivially, the total number of reflex, tangential, and convex vertices of $\mathcal{B}$ equals n.

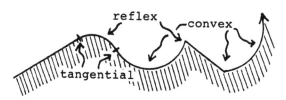

Figure 5.1: Convex, Tangential, and Reflex Objects.

5.2.2 Definition of the Voronoi Diagram

Definition 5.5 The *projection* of a point p onto an object o is a point $q \in \bar{o}$ s.t. $d(p,q) = d(p,o)$.

A projection needs not necessarily be well-defined. For instance, let o be a circular arc and ℓ the bisector of its endpoints. Furthermore, let r be the ray contained in ℓ that originates at the arc's center and does not intersect the arc. Obviously, every $p \in r$ is as close to the left endpoint of o as to its right endpoint.

Definition 5.6 A point p is *uniquely projectable* onto o if there exists at most one $q \in \bar{o}$ s.t. $d(p,o) = d(p,q)$ and $\ell(p,q)$ is normal on o.

By convention, every line is normal on a point. However, we will not be interested in projecting any point of the whole universe on any object. In the following, we define the interesting set.

Definition 5.7 The *cone of influence* $CI(o)$ of

- a circular arc o is the closure of the cone bounded by the pair of rays originating in the center of o and extending through the endpoints of o.

- a straight line segment o is the closure of the strip bounded by the normals through the endpoints of o.

- a point o is the whole plane.

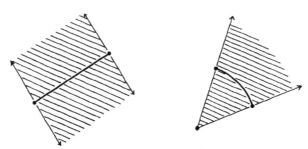

Figure 5.2: Cones of Influence.

Fig. 5.2 depicts the cones of influence for a line and an arc.

Lemma 5.1 Every $p \in CI(o)$ is uniquely projectable onto o, except for the center if o is a circular arc.

Interestingly, a lot of published definitions of Voronoi diagrams suffer from inadequacies with respect to the common understanding of Voronoi diagrams. Clearly, an inproper definition torpedos any proof of correctness.

For instance, a bisector is often defined as the locus of points equidistant from two objects, cf. Lee [Lee82] and Srinivasan and Nackman [SN87]. However, in the case of a straight line segment s and a vertex $p \in \bar{s}$, when using this definition the bisector is no longer one-dimensional. Rather, the bisector would be given by the half-space bounded by the normal on s through p, cf. Fig. 5.3.

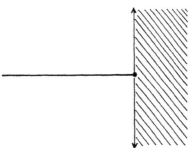

Figure 5.3: Two-dimensional 'Bisector'.

In order to avoid this difficulty, Yap [Yap85,Yap87] deals with ϵ-neighbourhoods. We simply restrict to the cone of influence.

Definition 5.8 For sets O_1, O_2, a point p is said to be *close* to O_1 w.r.t. O_2 if there exists an $o \in O_1$ s.t. $p \in CI(o)$ and $d(p, o) \leq d(p, O_2)$.

Definition 5.9 (Voronoi Region) The *Voronoi region* $\mathcal{VR}(O_1, O_2)$ of O_1 w.r.t. O_2 is given by $\mathcal{VR}(O_1, O_2) := \bigcup_{o \in O_1} \{ p \in CI(o) : d(p, o) \leq d(p, O_2) \}$.

Thus, $\mathcal{VR}(O_1, O_2)$ is the locus of all points that are close to O_1 w.r.t. O_2. Restricting O_1 to a single object, we get the definition of a Voronoi area.

Definition 5.10 (Voronoi Area) The *Voronoi area* $\mathcal{VA}(o, O)$ of o w.r.t. O is given by $\mathcal{VA}(o, O) := \{p \in CI(o) : d(p, o) \le d(p, O)\}$.

Thus, $\mathcal{VA}(o, O)$ is the locus of all points that are close to o w.r.t. O.

Definition 5.11 (Bisector) The *bisector* $b(o_1, o_2)$ between two objects o_1, o_2 is given by $b(o_1, o_2) := \{p \in CI(o_1) \cap CI(o_2) : d(p, o_1) = d(p, o_2)\}$.

Thus, $b(o_1, o_2)$ is the locus of all points p that are close to both, o_1 w.r.t. o_2 and o_2 w.r.t. o_1.

Definition 5.12 For a point p, objects o_1, o_2, and a set O,

closer $(p, o_1, o_2, O) :\Longleftrightarrow$

$$p \in CI(o_1) \cap CI(o_2) \ \wedge \ d(p, o_1) = d(p, o_2) \le d(p, O).$$

Definition 5.13 The *bisector* $b(O_1, O_2)$ between two sets of objects O_1, O_2 is given by $b(O_1, O_2) := \bigcup_{o_1 \in O_1, o_2 \in O_2} \{p : \text{closer } (p, o_1, o_2, O_1 \cup O_2)\}$.

Thus, $b(O_1, O_2)$ is the locus of all points p that are close to both, O_1 w.r.t. O_2 and O_2 w.r.t. O_1.

Definition 5.14 (Voronoi Polygon) For a set O and $o \in O$, the *Voronoi polygon* $\mathcal{VP}(o, O)$ of o w.r.t. O is the bisector $b(o, O \setminus \{o\})$.

Definition 5.15 (Voronoi Diagram) The *Voronoi diagram* $\mathcal{VD}(O)$ of a set O is given by $\mathcal{VD}(O) = \{p : (\exists\, o_1 \ne o_2 \in O) \text{ s.t. closer } (p, o_1, o_2, O)\}$.

Thus, $\mathcal{VD}(O)$ is the locus of points that are close to at least two disjoint objects of the set O.

5.2.3 Basic Facts about Voronoi Diagrams

The following definitions and lemmata are helpful for carrying out the correctness proofs of our algorithms. For the sake of shortness, proofs of lemmata that are either very easy or similar to other stated proofs are omitted. Furthermore, within the different settings, proof sketches can often be found in the published literature on Voronoi diagrams. However, care has to be taken whether the defined Voronoi diagram is correctly reflected by the stated properties.

Lemma 5.2 Let s be a segment, s not a point.

- For every $p \in \underline{CI(s)}$, $d(p, s) < d(p, \bar{s} \setminus \{s\})$.
- For every $p \in \complement\underline{CI(s)}$, $d(p, s) = d(p, \bar{s} \setminus \{s\})$.

Lemma 5.3 For disjoint complete sets O_1, O_2, a point p is close to O_1 w.r.t. O_2 iff there exists an $o \in O_1$ s.t. p is close to o w.r.t. $O_1 \cup O_2$.

Proof:

1) Trivially, for $o \in O_1$, if p is close to o w.r.t. $O_1 \cup O_2$, then p is close to O_1 w.r.t. O_2.

2) Let p be close to O_1 w.r.t. O_2. Suppose that, for an $o \in O_1$ with $d(p, o) \leq d(p, O_1)$, $p \in CI(o)$. Then, p is close to o w.r.t. $O_1 \cup O_2$.

Hence, suppose that $p \notin CI(o)$. Obviously, o cannot be a point. Since O_1 is complete, $\bar{o} \setminus \{o\} \in O_1$. Furthermore, by Lemma 5.2, $d(p, \bar{o} \setminus \{o\}) = d(p, O_1)$. Hence, p is close to one of the endpoints of o (w.r.t. $O_1 \cup O_2$). $\qquad\square$

Lemma 5.4 For a set O and $o \in O$, $\mathcal{VA}(o, O) = \bigcap_{o_1 \in O \setminus \{o\}} \mathcal{VA}(o, o_1)$.

Lemma 5.5 For sets O_1, O_2, $\mathcal{VR}(O_1, O_2) = \bigcup_{o_1 \in O_1} \mathcal{VA}(o_1, O_2)$.

Lemma 5.6 For a point p, objects o_1, o_2, and a set O,

$$\text{closer } (p, o_1, o_2, O) \iff p \in \mathcal{VA}(o_1, O) \cap \mathcal{VA}(o_2, O).$$

Lemma 5.7 The Voronoi diagram $\mathcal{VD}(O)$ is the union of its Voronoi polygons, i.e. $\mathcal{VD}(O) = \bigcup_{o \in O} \mathcal{VP}(o, O)$.

Proof:

$$
\begin{aligned}
\mathcal{VD}(O) &= \{p : (\exists\, o_1 \neq o_2 \in O) \text{ s.t. closer } (p, o_1, o_2, O)\} \\
&= \bigcup_{o_1 \neq o_2 \in O} \{p : \text{closer } (p, o_1, o_2, O)\} \\
&= \bigcup_{o_1 \in O} \bigcup_{o_2 \in O \setminus \{o_1\}} \{p : \text{closer } (p, o_1, o_2, O)\} \\
&= \bigcup_{o_1 \in O} b(o_1, O \setminus \{o_1\}) \\
&= \bigcup_{o_1 \in O} \mathcal{VP}(o_1, O).
\end{aligned}
$$

$\qquad\square$

Lemma 5.8 For $o \in O$, $VP(o, O) \subseteq \bigcup_{o_1 \in O \setminus \{o\}} b(o, o_1)$.

Definition 5.16 For a set O and $o \in O$, the collection $E(VP(o, O))$ of *edges* between o and $O \setminus \{o\}$ is defined as

$$E(VP(o, O)) := \bigcup_{o_1 \in O \setminus \{o\}} \{e \subseteq VP(o, O) \cap b(o, o_1) : e \text{ is maximal}\},$$

where e is *maximal* (w.r.t. O, o, o_1) if $e \neq \emptyset$ and e is not a point and if no larger path-connected subset of $VP(o, O) \cap b(o, o_1)$ exists that contains e.

Definition 5.17 For a set O, the collection $E(VD(O))$ of *Voronoi edges* is defined as $E(VD(O)) := \bigcup_{o \in O} E(VP(o, O))$.

Lemma 5.9 Every edge $e \in E(VD(O))$ is a portion of a unique conic.

Proof: Recall that e lies within the cones of influence of its two defining objects. Hence, the proof can be carried out by a simple case analysis. □

Definition 5.18 The circle $C(p, d(p, O))$ is called the *clearance circle* of p w.r.t. O. Similarly, the disk $D(p, d(p, O))$ is called the *clearance disk* of p w.r.t. O.

Definition 5.19 For $p \in CI(o)$, the *clearance line (segment)* through p w.r.t. o is given by the line (segment) through p and the projection of p onto o.

Definition 5.20 A *profile* P is a simple curve consisting of objects.

Lemma 5.10 For every $o \in O$ and $p \in VA(o, O)$, the clearance line segment of p w.r.t. o is completely contained in $VA(o, O)$.

Proof: By a case analysis. Let $p \in VA(o, O)$ and let ℓ denote the clearance line segment of p w.r.t. o.
Case 1: o is a segment s. Let v_1, v_2 the vertices of s and suppose that $v_1 \in O$ and $p \in VA(s, O) \cap VA(v_1, O)$. For $q \in \ell$, $d(q, s) = d(q, v_1) < d(q, O \setminus \{s, v_1\})$. Hence, $\ell \subseteq VA(s, O) \cap VA(v_1, O)$.
Now, suppose that $p \in VA(s, O) \cap \complement[VA(v_1, O) \cup VA(v_2, O)]$, where $VA(v_i, O)$ equals $\emptyset$ if $v_i \notin O$. Let $q \in \ell$. Obviously, $q \in CI(s)$. Hence, if $q \notin VA(s, O)$ then $d(q, s) > d(q, O_s)$, where $O_s := O \setminus \{s\}$. By the triangle inequality,

$$d(p, O_s) \leq d(q, O_s) + d(p, q) < d(q, s) + d(p, q) = d(p, s).$$

This yields the contradiction $p \notin VA(s, O)$.
Case 2: o is a vertex v. Proof similar to case 1. □

Corollary 5.1 For a profile P and a set of objects O, $\mathcal{VR}(P,O)$ is generalized-star-shaped with nucleus $\overline{P}$.

Lemma 5.11 For a profile P and a set of objects O, $\mathcal{VR}(P,O)$ is path-connected.

Proof: Let $p_1 \neq p_2 \in \mathcal{VR}(P,O)$ and denote their projections onto $o_1, o_2 \in \overline{P}$ by p_{o_1}, p_{o_2}. Due to Lemma 5.10 and Lemma 5.5, the path from p along the clearance line segment of p to p_{o_1}, from p_{o_1} along P to p_{o_2}, and from p_{o_2} along the clearance line segment of p_2 to p_2 is completely contained in $\mathcal{VR}(P,O)$. $\square$

Lemma 5.12 Let $o \in O$. For $p \in \mathcal{VA}(o,O)$ and $O_o := O \setminus \{o_1 \in O : o \subseteq \overline{o_1}\}$, $d(p,o) < d(p,O_o)$.

Proof: Let ℓ_1 be the clearance segment of p w.r.t. o. Choose ρ s.t. $D(p,\rho) \subseteq \mathcal{VA}(o,O)$. Now, suppose that $d(p,O_o) \leq d(p,o)$ and let ℓ_2 the clearance segment of p w.r.t. to O_o. Let $q = C(p,\rho/2) \cap \ell_2$.
Case 1: ℓ_1 and ℓ_2 are contained in the same line. Due to the definition of O_o we note that $q \notin \ell_1$. Hence,

$$d(q,O_o) < d(p,O_o) \leq d(p,o) < d(q,o).$$

This yields $d(q,O_o) < d(q,o)$, which is a contradiction to $q \in \mathcal{VA}(o,O)$.
Case 2: ℓ_1 and ℓ_2 are not contained in the same line. By the triangle inequality,

$$
\begin{aligned}
d(q,O_o) &= d(p,O_o) - d(p,q) = d(p,o) - d(p,q) \\
&< d(q,o) + d(p,q) - d(p,q) = d(q,o),
\end{aligned}
$$

which again yields the contradiction $d(q,O_o) < d(q,o)$. $\square$

Corollary 5.2 For a set O, the interiors of Voronoi areas of disjoint objects of O are disjoint.

Corollary 5.3 For a complete set O, every edge $e \in \mathcal{VD}(O)$ is shared by exactly two Voronoi polygons.

Corollary 5.4 For a set O, Voronoi edges do not intersect except in their endpoints.

Definition 5.21 The set $N(\mathcal{VD}(O))$ of *Voronoi nodes* is the set of points of $\mathcal{VD}(O)$ that belong to at least two Voronoi edges.

From the last corollary, it follows that the Voronoi nodes are the endpoints of Voronoi edges.

Lemma 5.13 For $o \in O$, let $p \neq q \in \mathcal{VA}(o, O)$. Then, either the clearance line segment of p w.r.t. o totally contains the clearance segment of q w.r.t. o (or vice versa), or the clearance segments do not intersect (except possibly at their endpoints).

Proof: Denote the projections of p and q onto o by p_o and q_o. Suppose that none of the two clearance segments contains the other but they intersect in a, with $a \notin o$. W.l.o.g. assume that $d(a, q_o) \leq d(a, p_o)$. Then, by the triangle inequality,

$$d(p, q_o) < d(p, a) + d(a, q_o) \leq d(p, a) + d(a, p_o) = d(p, p_o).$$

This yields a contradiction to p_o being the projection of p onto o. $\square$

Lemma 5.14 For a complete set O, every $v \in N(\mathcal{VD}(O))$ is at least of degree three.

Proof: Suppose that only two edges e_1, e_2 are incident upon a node v. Obviously, e_1 and e_2 are shared by the same objects $o_1 \neq o_2 \in O$. Hence, $e_1 \cup e_2$ form a portion of the bisector $b(o_1, o_2)$, contradicting the maximality of the Voronoi edges. $\square$

Definition 5.22 For a complete set O, the *dual graph* $\mathcal{D}(O)$ is the graph with nodes each of which corresponds to one object of O, and with edges interconnecting nodes whose associated Voronoi areas share an edge.

Due to Corollary 5.3, there exists a one-to-one correspondence between edges of $\mathcal{D}(O)$ and edges of $\mathcal{VD}(O)$.

Lemma 5.15 For a complete set O of $n \geq 3$ objects, $\mathcal{VD}(O)$ has at most $2n - 5$ nodes and $3n - 6$ edges.

Proof: We construct a planar embedding of $\mathcal{D}(O)$ and use Euler's Formula afterwards for obtaining bounds on the number of edges and faces of $\mathcal{D}(O)$.
First, for each $o \in O$ we choose an arbitrary representative $p_o \in o$. Similarly, for each $e \in E(\mathcal{VD}(O))$, we choose a representative $p_e \in \underline{e}$. Let $q(p_e, o)$ denote the projection of p_e onto o. Observe that the projection is well defined. Now, for $e \in E(\mathcal{VP}(o', O)) \cap E(\mathcal{VP}(o'', O))$, o' and o'' can be interconnected by the line segments between $q(p_e, o')$ and p_e, on one hand, and between p_e and $q(p_e, o'')$,

on the other hand. This path can be extended to a path between $p_{o'}$ and $p_{o''}$ by moving along o' between $p_{o'}$ and $q(p_e, o')$, and by moving along o'' between $p_{o''}$ and $q(p_e, o'')$. Due to Lemma 5.13, all these paths do not intersect pairwise except for sharing portions on the objects of O. By a simple perturbation, we can achieve that all these paths do not intersect pairwise except for their endpoints. Hence, we conclude that $\mathcal{D}(O)$ is a planar graph.

Due to Lemma 5.14, every bounded face of $\mathcal{D}(O)$ is limited by at least three edges, and due to Corollary 5.3, every edge contributes to exactly two faces. Hence, we have $2|E| \geq 3|F|$ and $|N| = n$. By Euler's formula, $\mathcal{D}(O)$ has at most $3n - 6$ edges and at most $2n - 4$ faces. However, only the bounded faces dualize to nodes of $\mathcal{VD}(O)$. Hence, $\mathcal{VD}(O)$ has at most $3n - 6$ edges and at most $2n - 5$ nodes.   □

Theorem 5.1 For a proper set $\mathcal{B}(\mathcal{P})$ of n segments, k reflex vertices, and $n - k$ tangential and convex vertices, $\mathcal{VD}(\mathcal{B}) \cap \mathcal{P}$ has at most $n + k - 2$ nodes and $2(n + k) - 3$ edges.

Proof: According to the following Lemma 5.16, only reflex vertices contribute to $\mathcal{VD}(\mathcal{B}) \cap \mathcal{P}$. Hence, we conclude that $2|E| \geq 3(|F| - 1) + n + k$ and $|N| = n + k$. Again by Euler's Formula, the dual graph of the restricted Voronoi diagram has at most $2(n+k) - 3$ edges and at most $n + k - 1$ faces. However, only the bounded faces dualize to nodes of $\mathcal{VD}(O)$. Hence, $\mathcal{VD}(\mathcal{B}) \cap \mathcal{P}$ has at most $2(n + k) - 3$ edges and at most $n + k - 2$ nodes.   □

Let $\mathcal{B}_r$ denote $\mathcal{B}$ minus all tangential and convex vertices. Omitting the convex and tangential vertices is justified by the following lemma:

Lemma 5.16 $\mathcal{VD}(\mathcal{B}_r) \cap \mathcal{P} = \mathcal{VD}(\mathcal{B}) \cap \mathcal{P}$.

Proof: By a case analysis. Let v be a convex or tangential vertex and let s_1, s_2 be the segments incident upon v.

Case 1: v is a convex vertex. Observe that, for every point $p \in \mathcal{P}$, $d(p, \mathcal{B} \setminus \{v\}) < d(p, v)$. Hence v does not contribute to $\mathcal{VD}(\mathcal{B}) \cap \mathcal{P}$.

Case 2: v is a tangential vertex. For every point $p \in \mathcal{P}$, $d(p, \mathcal{B}) \leq d(p, v)$, because v is in the closure of s_1 and s_2. Hence, the points close to p are also close to s_1 or s_2. Thus, the contribution of v to $\mathcal{VD}(\mathcal{B}) \cap \mathcal{P}$ is totally contained in the contribution of s_1, s_2.   □

5.3 Computing $\mathcal{VD}(\mathcal{C}_0)$

In this section, we explain how to compute the Voronoi diagram of the proper boundary $\mathcal{C}_0$ of (the closure of) an admissible simply-connected pocket $\mathcal{P}$. After understanding how $\mathcal{VD}(\mathcal{C}_0)$ can be constructed, it will be easy to understand the construction of $\mathcal{VD}(\mathcal{C}_i)$ for $i \in \{1, \ldots, m\}$. Constructing $\mathcal{VD}(\mathcal{B})$ out of the individual diagrams $\mathcal{VD}(\mathcal{C}_i)$ is explained in the next section.

For shorthand, we abbreviate $\mathcal{C}_0$ to $\mathcal{C}$. Furthermore, we restrict the Voronoi diagram to $\mathcal{P}$. Thus, henceforth $\mathcal{VD}(\mathcal{C})$ means $\mathcal{VD}(\mathcal{C}) \cap \mathcal{P}$. Similarly, Voronoi diagrams, Voronoi polygons, bisectors, cones of influence, etc. defined by profiles $P \subseteq \mathcal{C}$ are restricted to the left side of P. As usual, n denotes the total number of segments of $\mathcal{C}$ and k stands for the total number of reflex vertices.

5.3.1 Preparing for the Voronoi Algorithm

We start with an informal discussion of our Voronoi algorithm. Our algorithm constitutes a generalization of the algorithm investigated by Lee and Drysdale for the construction of the Voronoi diagram in the interior of a simple polygon, see [LD81,Lee82].

Their main idea is to compute $\mathcal{VD}(\mathcal{C})$ by applying a divide-and-conquer technique. This means that $\mathcal{VD}(\mathcal{C})$ is 'merged' from the precomputed diagrams $\mathcal{VD}(P_L)$ and $\mathcal{VD}(P_R)$, where P_L, P_R are disjoint profiles (except for their endpoints) that together form up $\mathcal{C}$. Similarly, for $i \in \{L, R\}$, $\mathcal{VD}(P_i)$ is recursively computed from the diagrams $\mathcal{VD}(P_{i1})$ and $\mathcal{VD}(P_{i2})$ of the two subprofiles P_{i1} and P_{i2} of P_i.

The construction of the Voronoi diagram $\mathcal{VD}(\mathcal{C})$ resembles a binary tree, the nodes of which correspond to this divide and subsequent conquer of profiles and their associated Voronoi diagrams. As a matter of fact, the leaves of the tree could be the individual contour objects. Assuming that the total time spent for processing the merge at one height level of the tree is equal to $O(n)$, we would get an overall running time of $O(n \log n)$ for recursively computing the Voronoi diagram $\mathcal{VD}(\mathcal{C})$, because a height-balanced binary tree with $O(n)$ leaves has height $O(\log n)$.

One can do slightly better. Assume that the Voronoi diagrams of the profiles $P_1, \ldots, P_l$ are available in time $O(n)$, with $\mathcal{C} = \cup_{1 \le i \le l} P_i$. By letting these profiles be the leaves of the merge tree, the Voronoi diagram could be iteratively computed in time $O(n \log l)$.

This modification, which has been suggested by Lee and Drysdale, does clearly not improve the overall worst-case time behaviour of the algorithm. But our own implementation witnessed a significant decrease of the computation time. A heuristic analysis convinced us that this preprocessing has the beneficial side-effect of avoiding a considerably large amount of redundant computations. The following definition is used for establishing a reasonable set of leaves.

Definition 5.23 The profile $P \subseteq C$ is called *reflex* if P does not contain any convex arc or convex vertex. A reflex profile is called *maximal* if adding additional objects at the beginning or the end of the profile causes the profile not to be reflex any more.

Lemma 5.17 Maximal reflex profiles of C do not intersect.

Proof: Suppose that two maximal reflex profiles $P_1 \neq P_2 \subseteq C$ intersect. Since C is simple, an intersection can only occur if P_1, P_2 are consecutive and if some objects are shared by both, P_1 and P_2. However, in this case linking P_1 and P_2 would generate a larger profile, which yields a contradiction to the maximality of the profiles P_1 and P_2. $\square$

Definition 5.24 The sequence $S(C) = (P_1, \ldots, P_l)$ of *leaves of the merge tree* is a sequence of disjoint profiles P_i s.t.

1. for $1 \leq i \leq l$, $P_i \subseteq C$,

2. $\cup_{1 \leq i \leq l} P_i = C$,

3. every maximal reflex profile of C is contained in $S(C)$,

4. for $1 \leq i \leq l$, if P_i is no maximal reflex profile, then P_i is a single segment or a single vertex.

5. when moving along C, for $1 \leq i \leq l$, P_{i+1} is the CCW successor of P_i, which is denoted by $P_i \to P_{i+1}$.

Hence, $S(C)$ is a subdivision of C into the maximal reflex profiles and into the missing objects not being members of any reflex profile. Furthermore, we note that $S(C)$ is a finite collection of profiles. By replacing consecutive pairs of profiles of $S(C)$ by their concatenation, the modified sequence $S^*(C)$ is derived from $S(C)$.

Definition 5.25 Let $C \subseteq \mathcal{C}$ be a curve (oriented CCW).

- For $p_1 \neq p_2 \in C$, a point $q \in C$ is *between* p_1 and p_2 if, when moving CCW along C, these three points appear in the sequence p_1, q, p_2.

- For $p \in C$, C consists of the subcurves left (C, p) and right (C, p), where left (C, p) contains the portion of C between its start and p, and right (C, p) contains the portion of C between p and its end.

5.3.2 Discussion of the Voronoi Algorithm

Let us now assume that $\mathcal{VD}(P_L)$ and $\mathcal{VD}(P_R)$ are available, cf. Fig. 5.4, where $P_L \to P_R \in S^*(\mathcal{C})$. Hence, the start of P_R is incident upon the end of P_L. We note that P_L, P_R need not obey to any further restrictions. In particular, both profiles may be concatenations of profiles out of the original collection $S(\mathcal{C})$. It is convenient to regard P_L and P_R as the left (right, respectively) profile.

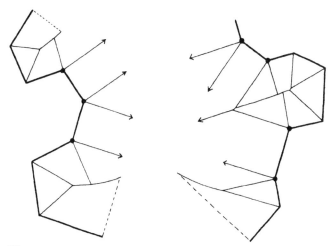

Figure 5.4: Voronoi Diagrams $\mathcal{VD}(P_L)$ and $\mathcal{VD}(P_R)$.

In the following, we will move along P_R in CCW order and along P_L in CW order. If a tangential or convex vertex is encountered during this move, we proceed to its successor in the specific moving direction.

Let $o_L \in P_L$ the end object of P_L and let $o_R \in P_R$ the start object of P_R. Then, as depicted in Fig. 5.5, $\mathcal{VD}(P_L \cup P_R)$ can be determined from $\mathcal{VD}(P_L)$ and $\mathcal{VD}(P_R)$ by means of the following merge process: Compute the bisector $b(o_L, o_R)$ and determine its intersections with $\mathcal{VP}(o_L, P_L)$ and $\mathcal{VP}(o_R, P_R)$. If the edge $e_L \in \mathcal{VP}(o_L, P_L)$ is intersected in q before $\mathcal{VP}(o_R, P_R)$ is intersected or if $\mathcal{VP}(o_R, P_R)$ is not at all intersected, then let the new o_L be the second defining object of e_L, i.e. that object whose Voronoi polygon shares e_L with the Voronoi polygon of the old o_L. Symmetrically, o_R is otherwise updated. Additionally, (the new) o_L and o_R are shrinked to left (o_L, q_{o_L}) and right (o_R, q_{o_R}), where q_{o_L} and q_{o_R} denote the projections of q onto o_L (o_R, respectively).

This merge process continues by computing the merge bisector $b(o_L, o_R)$ between the (new) defining objects o_L and o_R, by determining the first intersection of this bisector with $\mathcal{VP}(o_L, P_L)$ and $\mathcal{VP}(o_R, P_R)$, and by updating o_L and o_R. For one pair of defining contour objects, we call these three tasks a step. This merge process stops if

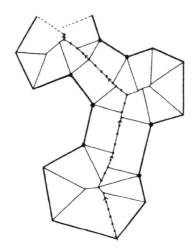

Figure 5.5: Merging $\mathcal{VD}(P_L)$ and $\mathcal{VD}(P_R)$.

1. either the first element of P_L or the last element of P_R has been reached and shrinked to a point,

2. or no further intersection of the merge bisector with the actual Voronoi polygons is reported.

After the end of the merge, a new profile is formed by concatenating P_L and P_R. Furthermore, the sequence $S^*(\mathcal{C})$ is updated by deleting P_L, P_R and inserting the new profile instead of them. Hence, $S^*(\mathcal{C})$ represents the entire contour $\mathcal{C}$ after the final Voronoi diagram $\mathcal{VD}(\mathcal{C})$ has been computed.

A straightforward implementation would scan the edges of a Voronoi polygon repeatedly if this Voronoi polygon is repeatedly encountered during the merge process. However, this simple approach may result in a quadratic worst-case behaviour. In order to improve the situation, the so-called Lee-Drysdale scan is applied, which in turn is based on the Shamos-Hoey scanning scheme.

As depicted in Fig. 5.6, suppose that the bisector b intersects $\mathcal{VP}(o_L, P_L)$ first in p. Then, no matter whether p is accepted or not, all (portions of) Voronoi edges of $\mathcal{VP}(o_L, P_L)$ lying to the right of b can be discarded. In other words, when scanning $\mathcal{VP}(o_L, P_L)$ in a CCW direction during the search for an intersection, no backtrack is needed. Since no edge of the left Voronoi regions (except for one per region) is scanned repeatedly, a linear number of edges of left Voronoi regions is scanned in total. Similarly, $\mathcal{VP}(o_R, P_R)$ is scanned in a CW direction.

The suitability of this approach heavily relies on the fact that every merge bisector $b(o_L, o_R)$ intersects both, $\mathcal{VP}(o_L, P_L)$ and $\mathcal{VP}(o_R, P_R)$. Unfortunately, this assumption is not true in our setting, and it seems that it is also not true within the settings of Lee, Drysdale, and Srinivasan and Nackman.

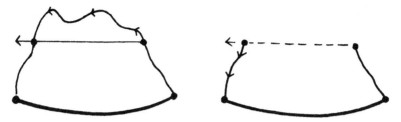

Figure 5.6: Lee-Drysdale Scan.

This flaw is eliminated by avoiding to scan the actual rest of a Voronoi polygon if no intersection occurs. As depicted in Fig. 5.7, two (chains of) bisectors sharing one defining object o can only intersect if their projections onto o overlap[3]. Fortunately, also a version of the other direction holds within our algorithm: if an overlap exists then some portions of bisectors can be discarded. Hence, only those bisectors are scanned that can be discarded.

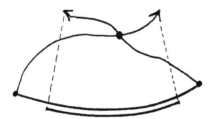

Figure 5.7: Projecting Two Chains of Bisectors.

This completes the description of our merge process for obtaining the Voronoi diagram $\mathcal{VD}(P_L \cup P_R)$ from the precomputed diagrams $\mathcal{VD}(P_L)$ and $\mathcal{VD}(P_R)$.

Those familiar with Lee's paper [Lee82] will have observed that our approach outlined above differs from Lee's approach mainly with respect to the following two aspects (besides the different definition of Voronoi diagrams):

1. Our method is a generalization of Lee's method to lines and arcs.

2. Computing bisectors between an endpoint of a profile and other objects is avoided. This usually results in significant practical savings of CPU-time, although it does not improve the overall worst-case complexity, which still is $O((n + k)\log(n + k))$.

---

[3]In case that the restriction to the cones of influence does not yield an upper bound on the parameter interval of a bisector, an upperbound can be artificially imposed by, for example, taking the length of the sides of a square inclosing the pocket.

5.4 Analysis of the Voronoi Algorithm

5.4.1 Termination of the Merge Process

Lemma 5.18 For $P_L \to P_R \in S^*(\mathcal{C})$, $b(P_L, P_R)$ is path-connected.

Proof: Let $p \neq q \in b(P_L, P_R)$ and denote their projections onto P_L by p_L, q_L (onto P_R by p_R, q_R, respectively). Recall the proof of Lemma 5.11: p and q can be linked by curves C_L, C_R entirely contained within $\mathcal{VR}(P_L, P_R)$, respectively $\mathcal{VR}(P_R, P_L)$. By inverting the direction of projection used in Lemma 5.10, C_L can continuously be deformed within $\mathcal{VR}(P_L, P_R)$ into a curve C^L that is contained in $\partial\mathcal{VR}(P_L, P_R)$. Similarly, C_R can continuously be deformed into $C^R \in \partial\mathcal{VR}(P_R, P_L)$. Observe that C^L, C^R are still path-connected.
Case 1: If $C^L = C^R$, then $C^L \subseteq b(P_L, P_R)$ and we are finished because p and q are connected by C^L.
Case 2: $C^L \neq C^R$. Since C^L, C^R share their endpoints, they bound at least one non-empty open area that neither belongs to $\mathcal{VR}(P_L, P_R)$ nor to $\mathcal{VR}(P_R, P_L)$. However, this cannot happen. $\square$

Lemma 5.19 For $P_L \to P_R \in S^*(\mathcal{C})$, $b(P_L, P_R)$ is a simple curve.

Proof: Suppose that $b(P_L, P_R)$ has a self-intersection. Hence, it contains a simple closed curve C. It is easy to understand that C has to enclose a non-empty open region. Again, this cannot happen. $\square$

Theorem 5.2 (Termination) For $P_L \to P_R \in S^*(\mathcal{C})$, the merge process for computing $\mathcal{VD}(P_L \cup P_R)$ from the precomputed diagrams $\mathcal{VD}(P_L)$ and $\mathcal{VD}(P_R)$ terminates.

Proof: By Theorem 5.1, $\mathcal{VD}(P_L)$, $\mathcal{VD}(P_R)$, and $b(P_L, P_R)$ consist of finitely many edges. Due to the previous Lemma 5.19, the number of edges in $b(P_L, P_R)$ equals the number of steps performed during the merge process. Since each step examines only a finite number of entities, the merge process terminates. $\square$

5.4.2 Correctness of the Merge Process

Lemma 5.20 For $P_L \to P_R \in S^*(\mathcal{C})$ and $P_{new} := P_L \cup P_R$, $\mathcal{VD}(P_{new})$ is given by

$$
\begin{aligned}
\mathcal{VD}(P_{new}) \;=\; & \mathcal{VD}(P_L) \cap \mathcal{VR}(P_L, P_R) \;\cup \\
& \mathcal{VD}(P_R) \cap \mathcal{VR}(P_R, P_L) \;\cup \\
& b(P_L, P_R).
\end{aligned}
$$

Proof: Since every Voronoi edge is shared by exactly two Voronoi polygons (areas, respectively), we obtain

$$
\begin{aligned}
\mathcal{VD}(P_{new}) &= \bigcup_{o_1 \neq o_2 \in P_{new}} \mathcal{VA}(o_1, P_{new}) \cap \mathcal{VA}(o_2, P_{new}) \\
&= \bigcup_{o_1 \neq o_2 \in P_L} \mathcal{VA}(o_1, P_{new}) \cap \mathcal{VA}(o_2, P_{new}) \quad \cup \\
&\quad\quad \bigcup_{o_1 \neq o_2 \in P_R} \mathcal{VA}(o_1, P_{new}) \cap \mathcal{VA}(o_2, P_{new}) \quad \cup \\
&\quad\quad \bigcup_{o_1 \in P_L, o_2 \in P_R} \mathcal{VA}(o_1, P_{new}) \cap \mathcal{VA}(o_2, P_{new}) \\
&\overset{*}{=} \bigcup_{o_1 \neq o_2 \in P_L} \mathcal{VA}(o_1, P_L) \cap \mathcal{VA}(o_2, P_L) \cap \mathcal{VR}(P_L, P_R) \quad \cup \\
&\quad\quad \bigcup_{o_1 \neq o_2 \in P_R} \mathcal{VA}(o_1, P_R) \cap \mathcal{VA}(o_2, P_R) \cap \mathcal{VR}(P_R, P_L) \quad \cup \\
&\quad\quad \bigcup_{o_1 \in P_L, o_2 \in P_R} \mathcal{VA}(o_1, P_{new}) \cap \mathcal{VA}(o_2, P_{new}) \\
&= \mathcal{VD}(P_L) \cap \mathcal{VR}(P_L, P_R) \quad \cup \\
&\quad\quad \mathcal{VD}(P_R) \cap \mathcal{VR}(P_R, P_L) \quad \cup \\
&\quad\quad b(P_L, P_R).
\end{aligned}
$$

Equality at $*$ holds due to the following fact: For $o \in P_L$,

$$
p \in \mathcal{VA}(o, P_{new}) \Longleftrightarrow p \in \mathcal{VA}(o, P_L) \cap V R(P_L, P_R).
$$

By symmetry, a similar relation holds for $o \in P_R$. □

In common words, this means that $\mathcal{VD}(P_L \cup P_R)$ consists of the merge curve $b(P_L, P_R)$ and of those portions of $\mathcal{VD}(P_L)$ and $\mathcal{VD}(P_R)$ that lie to the left (right, respectively) of the merge curve. Lemma 5.20 already settles the overall correctness of the divide-and-conquer approach. The following lemma reveals the correctness of the Lee-Drysdale scan, compare also [LD81].

Lemma 5.21 Let $b(o_L, o_R)$ be a bisector constructed during the merge process. If $b(o_L, o_R)$ intersects $\mathcal{VP}(o_L, P_L)$, then the first intersection is found by scanning $\mathcal{VP}(o_L, P_L)$ in a CCW direction. Similarly, $\mathcal{VP}(o_R, P_R)$ has to be scanned in a CW direction.

Proof: Let p be the intersection between $b(o_L, o_R)$ and $\mathcal{VP}(o_L, P_L)$ encountered first when scanning $\mathcal{VP}(o_L, P_L)$ in a CCW manner. Suppose that there exists an intersection q such that the projection of q onto o_L is between the projection of p onto o_L and the actual endpoint of o_L. In this case, $\mathcal{VP}(o_L, P_L)$ must twice intersect the clearance line segment of p w.r.t. o_L. However, this is not possible because the clearance segment is completely contained in $\mathcal{V}\mathcal{A}(o_L, P_L)$, recall Lemma 5.10. $\qquad\square$

Theorem 5.3 During the merge process, exactly those portions of $\mathcal{V}\mathcal{D}(P_L)$ and $\mathcal{V}\mathcal{D}(P_R)$ are discarded that are no members of $\mathcal{V}\mathcal{D}(P_{new})$. Furthermore, the remaining portions of $\mathcal{V}\mathcal{D}(P_L)$ and $\mathcal{V}\mathcal{D}(P_R)$ together with $b(P_L, P_R)$ form $\mathcal{V}\mathcal{D}(P_{new})$.

Proof: The theorem follows immediately the Lemmata 5.20 and 5.21. $\qquad\square$

5.4.3 Worst-case Analysis of the Voronoi Algorithm

The following lemma implies that, for $1 \leq i \leq l$ and $P_i \in S(\mathcal{C})$, $\mathcal{V}\mathcal{D}(P_i)$ can be obtained in time linear in the number of objects contained in P_i.

Lemma 5.22 For $P \in S(\mathcal{C})$, if $\mathcal{V}\mathcal{D}(P)$ is not empty then $\mathcal{V}\mathcal{D}(P)$ is given by the bisectors between consecutive objects of P. Furthermore, each bisector is a straight line (segment) and bisectors do not intersect pairwise (except possibly in their endpoints).

Proof: Suppose that $\mathcal{V}\mathcal{D}(P)$ is not empty. Hence, P is a maximal reflex profile. By a simple case analysis, it is clear that each bisector is a portion of a straight line normal on its defining contour objects (because P does not contain convex vertices). Furthermore, since P does not contain convex arcs, bisectors[4] do not intersect pairwise (except possibly in their endpoints). $\qquad\square$

In order to be able to state the worst-case complexity of the merge process, we have to analyze our scheme for intersecting and discarding bisectors.

Definition 5.26 For an object o, assume that a point $p \in CI(o)$ and a curve $C \in CI(o)$ are arranged such that the clearance line of p w.r.t. o intersects C exactly once. Then, p is said to be *below* C if the clearance line segment of p w.r.t. o does not intersect C, and *above* otherwise.

Lemma 5.23 Suppose that $b_2 = b(o_L, o_R)$ has been constructed during merging $\mathcal{V}\mathcal{D}(P_L)$ and $\mathcal{V}\mathcal{D}(P_R)$. Let C be (the actual rest of) $\mathcal{V}\mathcal{P}(o_L, P_L)$ and denote the bisector incident upon the endpoint p of C by b_1. Furthermore, suppose that the projections of b_1 and b_2 onto o_L overlap.

---

[4] Identical bisectors incident upon a tangential vertex are treated as one single bisector.

1. If p is below b_2 then that portion of b_2 which lies to the left of the clearance line of p w.r.t. o_L can be discarded.

2. Otherwise, intersect b_1 and b_2.

   a) If an intersection exists then that portion of b_1 between the end of b_1 and the point of intersection can be discarded.

   b) If no intersection exists then that portion of b_1 that lies above b_2 can be discarded. If b_2 is totally discarded then the next bisector of b_1 CCW along C has to be examined.

Proof:
Case 1: Follows from Lemma 5.10 and Lemma 5.4.
Case 2a: Follows from Lemma 5.4.
Case 2b: Follows from Lemma 5.10 and Lemma 5.4. $\square$

Lemma 5.24 The merge process for computing $\mathcal{VD}(P_{new})$ from $\mathcal{VD}(P_L)$ and $\mathcal{VD}(P_R)$ takes $O(n_L + k_L + n_R + k_R)$ time, where n_L, k_L and n_R, k_R denote the total number of segments and reflex vertices in P_L (in P_R, respectively).

Proof: Due to Lemma 5.16, convex and tangential vertices do not contribute to $\mathcal{VD}(P_L)$, $\mathcal{VD}(P_R)$, and $b(P_L, P_R)$. According to the preceding Lemma 5.23, at each step of the merge only those bisectors of the actual left Voronoi polygon are examined that can be discarded. Additionally, the very last bisector is examined. Since there are $O(n_L + k_L)$ bisectors in the left diagram $\mathcal{VD}(P_L)$, at most this number of bisectors can be discarded in the left diagram. By symmetry, a similar analysis holds for the right diagram $\mathcal{VD}(P_R)$. Furthermore, the number of examined last bisectors is linear in the number of bisectors contained in the merge curve. Hence, we come up with the stated upper bound. $\square$

Theorem 5.4 (Complexity of Computing $\mathcal{VD}(C)$) The divide-and-conquer algorithm presented above determines the Voronoi diagram $\mathcal{VD}(C)$ in worst-case time $O((n + k) \cdot (1 + \log l))$, where n denotes the number of segments, k stands for the number of reflex vertices, and $l \leq n$ denotes the initial number of profiles of $S(C)$.

Proof: Due to Lemma 5.16, convex and tangential vertices can be omitted without practical harm[5]. This establishes the inequality $l \leq n$. The rest follows from the preceding lemma and the fact that a binary merge tree is used. $\square$

---

[5] However, the stated proofs become much more complicated because the profiles of $S^*(C)$ are no longer (path-connected) curves.

5.5   Computing $\mathcal{VD}(\mathcal{B})$

In this section, we explain how to compute the Voronoi diagram of the proper boundary $\mathcal{B}$ of (the closure of) an admissible multiply-connected pocket $\mathcal{P}$. We presuppose that, for $i \in \{0, \ldots, m\}$, the single Voronoi diagrams $\mathcal{VD}(\mathcal{C}_i)$ are available. Then, $\mathcal{VD}(\mathcal{B})$ is iteratively computed by merging $\mathcal{VD}(\mathcal{C}_{i+1})$ with $\mathcal{VD}(\cup_{1 \leq j \leq i} \mathcal{C}_j)$. We note that Theorem 5.4 implies that the Voronoi diagram in the exterior of a convex island can be constructed in linear time.

As stated by Lee and Drysdale [LD81], care has to be taken that the resulting merge curves are not broken up into several pieces. This problem may arise if the convex hull of one island contour is totally contained in the convex hull of another island contour. Hence, a careful ordering of the island contours is necessary. A detailed explanation of the subsequent algorithms can be found in the publication of Srinivasan and Nackman [SN87]. The companion paper [MS87] by Meshkat and Sakkas describes some aspects of the implementation. Hence, we content ourselves to a rough survey.

Suppose that the island contours are ordered such that, for $i \in \{1, \ldots, m-1\}$, $Y(\mathcal{C}_{i+1}) \leq Y(\mathcal{C}_i)$, where $Y(\mathcal{C})$ denotes the y-coordinate of the topmost point of $\mathcal{C}$.

Lemma 5.25 For $i \in \{0, \ldots, m-1\}$, the bisector $b(\mathcal{C}_{i+1}, \cup_{0 \leq j \leq i} \mathcal{C}_j)$ is a simple closed curve.

Proof: We refer to Srinivasan and Nackman [SN87].   □

Lemma 5.26 For $i \in \{0, \ldots, m-1\}$, $\mathcal{C}_{old} := \cup_{1 \leq j \leq i} \mathcal{C}_j$, and $\mathcal{C}_{new} := \mathcal{C}_{old} \cup \mathcal{C}_{i+1}$, $\mathcal{VD}(\mathcal{C}_{new})$ is given by

$$\mathcal{VD}(\mathcal{C}_{new}) = \mathcal{VD}^*(\mathcal{C}_{old}) \cup b(\mathcal{C}_{old}, \mathcal{C}_{i+1}) \cup VD^*(\mathcal{C}_{i+1}),$$

where $\mathcal{VD}^*(\mathcal{C}_{old}) := \mathcal{VD}(\mathcal{C}_{old}) \cap \mathcal{VR}(\mathcal{C}_{old}, \mathcal{C}_{i+1})$ and $\mathcal{VD}^*(\mathcal{C}_{i+1}) := \mathcal{VD}(\mathcal{C}_{i+1}) \cap \mathcal{VR}(\mathcal{C}_{i+1}, \mathcal{C}_{old})$.

Proof: Similar to the proof of Lemma 5.20.   □

When merging the Voronoi diagrams of two profiles $P_L \to P_R$, it is naturally to start the merge curve in the end of P_L. Merging the Voronoi diagrams of two (sets of) contours is conceptually not different. However, a suitable start of the merge curve has to be investigated. Fortunately, a start can be found in $\mathcal{VA}(o_1, \mathcal{C}_{i+1})$, where $o_1 \in \mathcal{C}_{i+1}$ is an object that contains a point p with maximal y-coordinate $Y(o_1) = Y(\mathcal{C}_{i+1})$.

Lemma 5.27 For $o_1 \in \mathcal{C}_{i+1}$ and $p \in o_1$ as defined above, let r be the vertical ray normal on o_1 that originates at p. Then, for every object $o_2 \in \mathcal{C}_{old}$ and every point $q \in r \cap \mathcal{VA}(o_2, \mathcal{C}_{old})$,

$$q \in b(o_1, o_2) \iff q \in b(\mathcal{C}_{i+1}, \mathcal{C}_{old}).$$

Proof:
1) Suppose that $q \in b(o_1, o_2)$. Observe that $q \in \mathcal{VA}(o_1, \mathcal{C}_{i+1})$. Hence, $q \in CI(o_1) \cap CI(o_2)$ and $d(q, o_1) = d(q, o_2) \leq d(q, \mathcal{C}_{new})$, which implies $q \in b(\mathcal{C}_{old}, \mathcal{C}_{i+1})$.
2) Suppose that $q \in b(\mathcal{C}_{i+1}, \mathcal{C}_{old})$. Since $q \in \mathcal{VA}(o_2, \mathcal{C}_{old})$, $q \in \mathcal{VA}(o_2, \mathcal{C}_{i+1})$. Since $q \in r$, $q \in \mathcal{VA}(o_1, \mathcal{C}_{new})$. Hence, $q \in b(o_1, o_2)$. □

The lemma implies that a point q which is guaranteed to be an element of $b(\mathcal{C}_{i+1}, \mathcal{C}_{old})$ can be found by means of the following algorithm Start_Point:

1. Let $p' := p$ and determine $o_2 \in \mathcal{C}_{old}$ s.t. $p' \in \mathcal{VP}(o_2, \mathcal{C}_{old})$.

2. a) Compute the connected component $\overline{(p', p'')}$ of $r \cap \mathcal{VP}(o_2, \mathcal{C}_{old})$.
   b) Compute $q := b(o_1, o_2) \cap \overline{(p', p'')}$.
   c) If no intersection exists then let $p' := p''$ and determine $o_2 \in \mathcal{C}_{old}$ s.t. r enters $\mathcal{VA}(o_2, \mathcal{C}_{old})$. Then go to Step 2a.

Attention has to be paid to the case where r is incident upon a Voronoi vertex. The following lemma states the complexity of finding a startpoint of $b(\mathcal{C}_{i+1}, \mathcal{C}_{old})$.

Lemma 5.28 Algorithm Start_Point finds a startpoint of $b(\mathcal{C}_{i+1}, \mathcal{C}_{old})$ in time $O(n + k)$, where n denotes the total number of segments of $\mathcal{C}_{old}$ and k stands for the total number of reflex vertices.

Proof: The correctness of the algorithm follows from Lemma 5.27. The claimed complexity bound has been proved in [SN87]. However, observe that during the execution of Start_Point a Voronoi area $\mathcal{VA}(o_2, \mathcal{C}_{old})$ may be entered and left more than once. Hence, a modified version of the Lee-Drysdale scan has to be applied during searching for intersections between r and the Voronoi polygons in order to ensure that every edge of every Voronoi polygon is examined only a constant number of times. □

This detail of the proof is omitted in [SN87]. Besides, it is not clear whether the modifications carried out in their implemented version still guarantee to achieve the same worst-case complexity, cf. [MS87].

As a further detail, we would like to point out that one bisector may be intersected twice by the merge curve $b(\mathcal{C}_{i+1}, \mathcal{C}_{old})$. Similar to the correctness considerations for the Lee-Drysdale scan it is easy to understand that at most

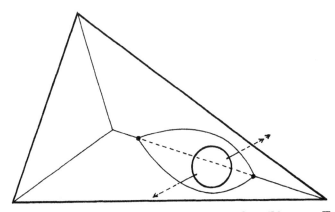

Figure 5.8: The Merge Curve May Intersect One Bisector Twice.

one bisector can be intersected twice by the merge curve. A double intersection happens iff $VD(C_{i+1}) \cap VD(C_{old} \cup C_{i+1})$ is contained in at most two Voronoi areas of $VD(C_{old})$, cf. Fig. 5.8. Hence, only the first bisector intersected by the merge curve can be intersected twice. After 'doubling' this bisector the conventional Lee-Drysdale scanning scheme can be applied.

We conclude the description of our approach to computing Voronoi diagrams with the final theorem that states the overall worst-case complexity.

Theorem 5.5 (Complexity of Computing $VD(\mathcal{B})$) For $0 \leq i \leq m$, let n_i and k_i denote the total number of segments (reflex vertices, respectively) contained in C_i. Besides, let l_i be the number of initial profiles contained in $S(C_i)$. Then, $VD(\mathcal{B}) = VD(\cup_{0 \leq i \leq m} C_i)$ can be computed in worst-case time

$$O(\sum_{i=0}^{m}(n_i + k_i) \cdot (1 + \log l_i) + \sum_{i=0}^{m-1} \sum_{j=0}^{i+1} n_j + k_j).$$

This is $O((n + k) \cdot (m + \log n))$, where $n := \sum_{i=0}^{m} n_i$ and $k := \sum_{i=0}^{m} k_i \leq n$.

Proof: Merging $VD(C_{i+1})$ and $VD(C_{old})$ takes time $\sum_{j=0}^{i+1} n_j + k_j$. The proof of this claim is conceptually not different from the proof of the Complexity Theorem 5.4, cf. [SN87]. The rest is an immediate consequence of Theorem 5.4.   □

Chapter 6

Implementational Issues

6.1   Representation of the Contours

Representing closed contours consisting of straight line segments and circular
arcs is fairly standard (if no sophisticated operations are required). The only
operations we would like to perform on the contours are

- obtaining information on the types and the coordinates of contour segments,

- 'walking' along the contours in a clockwise or counter-clockwise direction,

- inserting new contour segments.

It is quite natural to use a doubly-linked list for representing the contours.

In more detail this means that every contour object has two pointers
NextCCW and *NextCW* indicating the next object in CCW direction (in CW
direction, respectively). In order to store the coordinate values it is sufficient to
keep the object's starting point and the normalized direction of the object (in
the case of a straight line) or the object's center (in the case of a circular arc).
Reflex vertices are regarded as (degenerate) circular arcs with CW orientation.
Convex vertices may be omitted.

In the case of a circular arc, it is convenient to additionally store the circle's
radius because this value is often needed during computations. Besides, the radius
can be used for distinguishing between a vertex and a non-degenerate circle.
Furthermore, the flag *ccw_oriented* indicates the orientation of an arc.

We are aware that our representation scheme is not ultimate with respect
to the handling of circular arcs. For instance, storing the center, the endpoints,
and the radius of an arc introduces a lot of redundancy. Besides, circles of very
small curvature have a very large radius which may cause numerical problems.
This numerical problem may become particularly highlighted when dealing with
a sequence of arcs arising from the circular approximation of a curve exhibiting
small curvature.

As a matter of fact, both, the center (in the case of an arc) and the direction
(in the case of a line) could be omitted. Omitting the arc's center avoids the
redundancy but gives way to new numerical problems: For an arc approximately
equal to a semi-circle, small perturbations of the radius cause comparatively large
changes in the arc's actual shape. Besides, the numerical condition of determining
the center of a circular arc nearly equal to either a full circle or a vertex is bad,
too.

Motivated by these problems, in his Ph.D. thesis [Sab77], Sabin suggested to
describe a circular arc by means of its endpoints and by the ratio of the distance
perpendicular to the chord to half the length of the chord. Besides eliminating
redundancy and achieving numerical stability, this approach enables handling

straight line segments as circular arcs with zero curvature (at the expense of slightly more time-consuming operations). This possibility to reduce the total amount of separate algorithms for the handling of the individual types of contour elements should not be underestimated. However, Sabin's method is not capable of dealing with full circles or vertices as special cases of circular arcs.

6.2 Representation of the Bisectors

6.2.1 Parameterizing the Bisectors

Since the offset distance is widely used throughout GEOPOCKET, we have decided to express the bisectors as functions of their offset to the pocket boundary. This is exactly the approach suggested by Persson [Per78]. The striking advantage of this representation is the fact that the offset distance of a point lying on a bisector is given by its parameter value.

Before we can carry on with the parameterization formulas we have to be aware of the following problem: As depicted in Fig. 6.1, two points p_1, p_2 on a bisector b may have the same contour offset. Hence, b cannot be parameterized using the contour offset as parameter because this parameterization would not be single-valued.

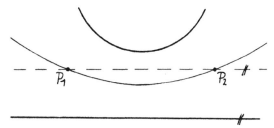

Figure 6.1: Points p_1, p_2 have the Same Offset.

Therefore, we have to be more specific when speaking of a 'bisector': we distinguish between

- *geometric bisectors*, i.e. the edges of the Voronoi diagram, and

- *analytic bisectors*, i.e. geometric bisectors split up at points of extreme offset distance.

When moving along an analytic bisector, the contour offset either monotonously increases or monotonously decreases. A simple case analysis shows that any geometric bisector at most splits up into two analytic bisectors.

How can we parameterize an analytic bisector? As depicted in Fig. 6.2, observe that the bisector between two objects o_1, o_2 has to pass through the intersection points of offset elements of o_1 and o_2. This idea is also known as applying a prairie fire to the pocket sides.

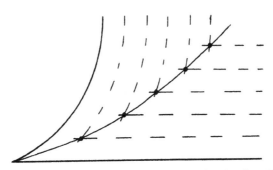

Figure 6.2: Applying a Prairie Fire to the Pocket Sides.

For the beginning, we do not distinguish between a bounded straight line segment and its supporting line, or between a circular arc and the circle the arc is a portion of. Lines and circles are specified by their implicit equational form. The equational form can easily be derived from our segment representation. Using the equational form, it is straightforward to specify offsets. Obviously, for a circle

$$(x - xc)^2 + (y - yc)^2 = r^2,$$

its offset circle (with offset t) is given by

$$(x(t) - xc)^2 + (y(t) - yc)^2 = (r + k \cdot t)^2,$$

where (xc, yc) denotes the circle's center and r stands for the circle's radius. By analogy, for a straight line

$$a \cdot x + b \cdot y + c = 0 \qquad \text{(with } a^2 + b^2 = 1),$$

the offset line is given by

$$a \cdot x(t) + b \cdot y(t) + c + k \cdot t = 0,$$

where a, b, c are the line's normalized coefficients. We assume that (a, b) stands for the inwards normal vector of the line.

In both formulas the sliding direction is given by $k = \pm 1$. The case $k = +1$ can be interpreted as enlarging a circle whereas $k = -1$ means to shrink its size. In the case of a straight line, k indicates whether the offset line is situated to the left or to the right of the line.

Now, the parameterization formulas for the bisectors (using the offset t as parameter) can be obtained by solving the intersection equations of the above stated offset elements with respect to x and y. As there is no principal difficulty in doing this job we do not carry out the calculations. Rather, we present the results. The following formulas have been first published by Persson [Per78].

Bisector Parameterizations:

straight line – straight line:

$$a_1 \cdot x(t) + b_1 \cdot y(t) + c_1 + k_1 \cdot t = 0 \ \wedge \ a_1^2 + b_1^2 = 1$$
$$a_2 \cdot x(t) + b_2 \cdot y(t) + c_2 + k_2 \cdot t = 0 \ \wedge \ a_2^2 + b_2^2 = 1$$

line bisector:

$$x(t) = (b_1 \cdot c_2 - b_2 \cdot c_1)/\Delta + t \cdot (b_1 \cdot k_2 - b_2 \cdot k_1)/\Delta$$
$$y(t) = (a_2 \cdot c_1 - a_1 \cdot c_2)/\Delta + t \cdot (a_2 \cdot k_1 - a_1 \cdot k_2)/\Delta$$
$$\Delta := a_1 \cdot b_2 - b_1 \cdot a_2$$

circle – straight line:

$$\big(x(t) - xc_1\big)^2 + \big(y(t) - yc_1\big)^2 = (r_1 + k_1 \cdot t)^2$$
$$a_2 \cdot x(t) + b_2 \cdot y(t) + c_2 + k_2 \cdot t = 0 \ \wedge \ a_2^2 + b_2^2 = 1$$

parabola bisector:

$$x(t) = xc_1 - a_2 \cdot h - k_2 \cdot a_2 \cdot t \pm b_2 \sqrt{r_1(t)^2 - h(t)^2}$$
$$y(t) = yc_1 - b_2 \cdot h - k_2 \cdot b_2 \cdot t \mp a_2 \sqrt{r_2(t)^2 - h(t)^2}$$
$$r_1(t) := r_1 + k_1 \cdot t$$
$$h := a_2 \cdot xc_1 + b_2 \cdot yc_1 + c_2$$
$$h(t) := h + k_2 \cdot t$$

circle – circle:

$$\big(x(t) - xc_1\big)^2 + \big(y(t) - yc_1\big)^2 = (r_1 + k_1 \cdot t)^2$$
$$\big(x(t) - xc_2\big)^2 + \big(y(t) - yc_2\big)^2 = (r_2 + k_2 \cdot t)^2$$

ellipse/hyperbola bisector:

$$x(t) = xc_1 - d_x \cdot h - d_x \cdot \Delta \cdot t \pm d_y \sqrt{r_1(t)^2 - h(t)^2}$$
$$y(t) = yc_1 - d_y \cdot h - d_y \cdot \Delta \cdot t \mp d_x \sqrt{r_1(t)^2 - h(t)^2}$$
$$r_1(t) := r_1 + k_1 \cdot t$$
$$r_2(t) := r_2 + k_2 \cdot t$$
$$d := \sqrt{(xc_1 - xc_2)^2 + (yc_1 - yc_2)^2}$$
$$d_x := (xc_2 - xc_1)/d$$
$$d_y := (yc_2 - yc_1)/d$$
$$\Delta := (k_2 \cdot r_2 - k_1 \cdot r_1)/d$$
$$h := (r_2^2 - r_1^2 - d^2)/2d$$
$$h(t) := (r_2(t)^2 - r_1(t)^2 - d^2)/2d$$

Summarizing, in this way the parameterization of a bisector can be computed undertaking few efforts. Note that the parameterizations of two analytic bisectors corresponding to one geometric bisector only differ by the sign of the square root. Hence, one analytic bisector is a portion of a line or circle, or one branch of a parabola, or one quarter of an ellipse or hyperbola.

But there exists a little problem: we have to remark that the above stated formulas only are valid if the defining objects are no parallel straight lines and no concentric circular arcs. Handling these degeneracies is conceptionally not very difficult and will be explained in Subsection 6.2.2. However, special cases cause most algorithms to get rather long and hard to understand.

The parameterization imposes a natural orientation on the analytic bisectors: Every analytic bisector originates at that endpoint which corresponds to the lower bound of its parameter interval and ends at that endpoint which corresponds to the upper bound of its parameter interval. Hence, when moving along an analytic bisector in accordance with its parameterization, the contour offset is (strictly) monotonously increasing. For bisectors defined by parallel lines or concentric arcs, the orientation can be chosen arbitrarily because they do not exhibit any change in the contour offset. In Chapter 7, we will make extensive use of this orientation of the bisectors.

In order to achieve a convenient representation of the bisectors we have also investigated some other parameterizations. In particular, we tried to avoid a different handling of bisectors in the non-degenerate and in the degenerate case. Anyway, parameterizations similar to the conventional parametric representations – e.g. $(a \cos \varphi, b \sin \varphi)$ for an ellipse – did not prove useful as we had great problems when trying to get the correct portion of the ellipse. Besides, these parameterizations lack any reasonable relation to the contour offset.

It is interesting to learn that none of the papers on Voronoi diagrams suggests a reasonable parameterization. Apart from Persson [Per78], this topic has not at all been treated in the published literature.

6.2.2 Storing the Bisector Parameterizations

On the previous pages, we have presented the parameterizations of the bisectors without stating in which way they can be stored. By inspection of the parameterizations we learn that the general formula for representing line-, parabola-, ellipse-, and hyperbola-bisectors is given by

$$x(t) = x_1 - x_2 - x_3 \cdot t \pm x_4 \cdot \sqrt{(x_5 + x_6 \cdot t)^2 - (x_7 + x_8 \cdot t)^2},$$

$$y(t) = y_1 - y_2 - y_3 \cdot t \mp y_4 \cdot \sqrt{(y_5 + y_6 \cdot t)^2 - (y_7 + y_8 \cdot t)^2},$$

where $(x_1, \ldots, x_8), (y_1, \ldots, y_8)$ denote the coefficient vectors depending on the bisector's defining objects.

As a matter of fact, one could simply store these vectors. However, when using 8 bytes per single value, storing both vectors would sum up to $\approx 0.12 KB$. Clearly, there is a trade-off between explicitly storing all bisector data and consuming a lot of storage, on one hand, and repeatedly recomputing most bisector data thereby saving storage, on the other hand. Nevertheless, since memory may be valuable when implementing our algorithm on a personal computer or within an NC, we have investigated a condensed representation of the bisectors.

GEOPOCKET makes use of four bisector data variables $\alpha_1, \ldots, \alpha_4$ (and an additional flag indicating the sign at the square root). Saving storage is possible because the parameterizing formulas contain values that can be extracted from the data on the bisector's defining objects rather than have to be stored explicitly.

In the following two tables, the defining objects of a bisector are denoted by using the abbreviations ℓ for line segment and c for circular arc. The indices 1 and 2 are used for indicating to which element a value corresponds. Table 6.1 summarizes the condensed representation of bisectors. Let $d := \sqrt{(xc_1 - xc_2)^2 + (yc_1 - yc_2)^2}$ and $\Delta := a_1 \cdot b_2 - a_2 \cdot b_1$. In the case of a CCW arc, $\lambda := -1$, and $\lambda := 1$ otherwise.

Condensed Representation		
Bisector	α_1	α_2
ℓ_1/ℓ_2	$(b_1 \cdot d_2 - b_2 \cdot d_1)/\Delta$	$(a_2 \cdot d_1 - a_1 \cdot d_2)/\Delta$
c_1/ℓ_2	a_2	b_2
c_1/c_2	$(xc_2 - xc_1)/d$	$(yc_2 - yc_1)/d$
Bisector	α_3	α_4
ℓ_1/ℓ_2	$b_2 - b_1$	$a_1 - a_2$
c_1/ℓ_2	$a_2 \cdot xc_1 + b_2 \cdot yc_1 + d_2$	r_1
c_1/c_2	$(r_2^2 - r_1^2 - d^2)/2d$	$(\lambda_2 \cdot r_2 - \lambda_1 \cdot r_1)/d$

Table 6.1: Condensed Representation of a Bisector.

Table 6.2 illustrates how to retrieve the complete coefficient vectors of the parameterization formulas from the condensed representation.

The condensed representation of bisectors can also be used for storing bisectors between parallel line segments or between concentric circular arcs. In these cases, the variables $\alpha_1, \ldots, \alpha_4$ simply contain the coordinates of the endpoints of such bisectors.

Coding the Parameterization Formulas								
Bisector	x_1	x_2	x_3	x_4	x_5	x_6	x_7	x_8
ℓ_1/ℓ_2	α_1	0	$-\alpha_3$	0	0	0	0	0
c_1/ℓ_2	xc_1	$\alpha_1 \cdot \alpha_3$	$-\alpha_1$	α_2	α_4	λ_1	α_3	-1
c_1/c_2	xc_1	$\alpha_1 \cdot \alpha_3$	$\alpha_1 \cdot \alpha_4$	α_2	r_1	λ_1	α_3	α_4
Bisector	y_1	y_2	y_3	y_4	y_5	y_6	y_7	y_8
ℓ_1/ℓ_2	α_2	0	$-\alpha_4$	0	0	0	0	0
c_1/ℓ_2	yc_1	$\alpha_2 \cdot \alpha_3$	$-\alpha_2$	α_1	α_4	λ_1	α_3	-1
c_1/c_2	yc_1	$\alpha_2 \cdot \alpha_3$	$\alpha_2 \cdot \alpha_4$	α_1	r_1	λ_1	α_3	α_4

Table 6.2: Obtaining the Complete Parameterization Formulas.

6.3 Representation of the Voronoi Diagram

6.3.1 Storing the Incidence Relations

After we have described the representation of a single (analytic) bisector we can think over a suitable data structure for representing the whole Voronoi diagram. Since the diagram can be regarded as a planar connected graph it is natural to analyze known graph representations. Common methods for storing a graph are using the *adjacency matrix* or the *edge lists*. The adjacency matrix represents a graph (having m nodes and e edges) by a boolean $m \times m$ matrix *adj_mat(i, j)* indicating whether there exists an edge from node i to node j. Clearly, the storage requirement of this representation is $\Theta(m^2)$. A more storage-efficient method is the use of edge lists: This means representing the graph by m lists where the ith list corresponds to the edges incident upon node i (arranged in the order which they appear as one proceeds CCW or CW around the node). The headers of each list can be stored in an array. This method consumes $O(m + e)$ storage.

As the Voronoi diagram has $O(n)$ nodes and edges one should not use the adjacency matrix because this would cause a waste of $O(n^2)$ storage. A linear storage requirement is guaranteed when using the edge lists. Besides, in this case it is trivial to obtain a sequence of edges incident upon a node. The disadvantage of this representation (with respect to our intended applications) is that all the information is concentrated in the nodes of the diagram and that it seems to be more difficult to get some information on entities such as Voronoi polygons.

For our purposes, a *winged-edge data structure* or a *doubly-connected edge list* (DCEL) is more appropriate. The winged-edge data structure has been introduced by Baumgart [Bau74,Bau75]; DCELs have been introduced by Muller and Preparata [MP78]. The basic ideas of these structures have recently been described by Mäntylä [Man88], and by Preparata and Shamos [PS88].

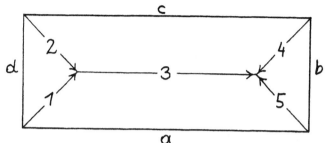

Figure 6.3: Voronoi Diagram Regarded as a Graph.

The main component of both data structures is the so-called edge node. In our application an edge node consists of six information fields: four pointers to those edges incident upon the actual edge's endnodes which are first encountered when proceeding around the endnodes in CCW or CW direction; and two pointers to the defining objects of the edge (i.e. bisector). By keeping pointers from the objects to the bisectors incident in their endpoints, the Voronoi diagram is linked with the boundary. Fig. 6.3 and Table 6.3 illustrate this representation scheme.

Doubly-Connected Edge List (DCEL)						
Edge	Tail_CCW	Tail_CW	Head_CCW	Head_CW	L_Face	R_Face
1	/	/	3	2	d	a
2	/	/	1	3	c	d
3	2	1	5	4	c	a
4	/	/	3	5	b	c
5	/	/	4	3	a	b

Table 6.3: DCEL of the Voronoi Diagram.

Summarizing, the objects of the contours and the edges of the Voronoi diagram are stored by means of the following two variant records *Object* and *Edge*. In Table 6.4, the tag field *line* is used for discriminating between straight line segments and circular arcs. In Table 6.5, the tag field *contour_bisector* is used for discriminating between bisectors originating at the contour, so-called *contour bisectors*, and those bisectors which do not originate at the contour, so-called *inner bisectors*.

type *Point* = **array** [1..2] **of LongReal**
type *Object_Ptr* = **pointer to** *Object*

type *Object* =
   record
      Next_CCW,Next_CW: *Object_Ptr*
      Starting_Point: *Point*
      case *line*: **Boolean of**
        true: *Direction*: *Point* |
        false: *Center*: *Point*
              Radius: **LongReal**
              ccw_oriented: **Boolean**
     end_case
   end_record

Table 6.4: Data Type *Object*.

type *Condensed_Bisector_Data* = **array** [1..4] **of LongReal**
type *Edge_Ptr* = **pointer to** *Edge*

type *Edge* =
   record
      Bisector_Data: *Condensed_Bisector_Data*
      Lower_Bound, Upper_Bound: **LongReal**
      case *contour_bisector*: **Boolean of**
        true: |
        false: *Tail_CCW, Tail_CW*: *Edge_Ptr*
     end_case
      Head_CCW,Head_CW: *Edge_Ptr*
      L_Face,R_Face: *Object_Ptr*
   end_record

Table 6.5: Data Type *Edge*.

6.3.2   On the Maximal Number of Analytic Bisectors

The question concerning the maximal number of analytic bisectors has been posed by Persson. In [Per], he gives an upper bound of $8n$ and depicts a worst-case example for $5n - O(1)$, where n denotes the total number of segments. This gap between the known maximal number of analytic bisectors and the assumed upper bound attracted our attention. In particular, when encoding our algorithms in a programming language that does not support dynamic storage allocation, such as FORTRAN 77, it is of some importance to know tight upper bounds on the storage needed.

Recall from Theorem 5.1 that the maximal number of geometric bisectors is given by $2(n+k)-3$, where k, as usual, denotes the total number of reflex vertices. Obviously, since every geometric bisector splits up into at most two analytic bisectors, this bound immediately implies the upper bound $2[2(n+k)-3] = 4(n+k)-6$ on the total number of analytic bisectors. This formula yields a total of $8n - O(1)$ analytic bisectors, as conjectured by Persson.

However, this bound is not tight. By a simple case analysis it is easy to see that the geometric contour bisectors incident upon reflex vertices are already analytic ones. Hence, they must not be counted twice. Furthermore, observe that there exist exactly $2k$ of these bisectors. These two observations lead to the following upper bound on the total number $\#_b(n)$ of analytic bisectors:

$$\#_b(n) \leq 4(n + k) - 6 - 2k = 4n + 2k - 6 \leq 6n - 6.$$

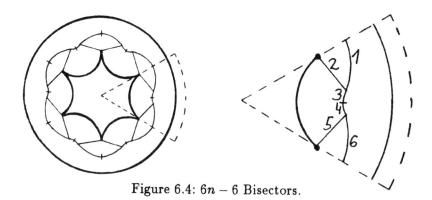

Figure 6.4: $6n - 6$ Bisectors.

Of course, one may wonder whether this bound is tight. Analyzing the upper bound $4n + 2k - 6$, we understand that any example illustrating the worst case must have $k \approx n$ reflex vertices. Furthermore, it is clear that all geometric bisectors except those incident upon reflex vertices have to split up into two analytic ones. Considering these two requirements we have designed the pocket depicted in Fig. 6.4: as it can be seen this pocket has $6n - 6$ analytic bisectors. Thus, we have proved the following lemma.

Lemma 6.1 For a pocket $\mathcal{P}$ with $\partial\mathcal{P}$ containing n segments, $\mathcal{VD}(\partial\mathcal{P})$ has at most $\#_b(n) = 6n - 6$ analytic bisectors, and this bound is tight.

6.4   Manipulating Bisectors

In the previous sections, we have explained how the data on metric and incidence relations of bisectors can be stored. In particular, we have stated the parameterization formulas for the conics envolved. However, we have not yet explained how to restrict to the correct portion of the conic and how to compute intersections amongst them.

6.4.1   Determining the Correct Portion of a Conic

Suppose that we are to compute a geometric bisector between two objects o_1, o_2 and already know one of its endpoints p (together with the offset t of p). This assumption is justified because when applying our algorithm one endpoint is either given by the common endpoint of the defining objects (in the case of a contour bisector), or by the last bisector intersection (in the case of an inner bisector).

After the parameterization formula of the supporting conic has been computed, p is used for determining the branch of the conic, i.e. the sign at the square root of the parameterization. This is executed by simply plugging t into the formula and comparing the computed result to p. In this way, the analytic bisector incident upon p is determined. Besides, t constitutes the lower bound (upper bound, respectively) of the bisector's parameter interval.

Then, the actual analytic bisector is restricted to the common cone of influence[1] of o_1 and o_2, i.e. to $CI(o_1) \cap CI(o_2)$. This task is executed by intersecting the analytic bisector with normals through the endpoints of o_1, o_2. If intersections are reported, the bisector is restricted and the computed intersection offset serves for establishing the second parameter bound. In this case, the second half of the conic is not needed, i.e. the geometric bisector between o_1 and o_2 is given by the actual analytic bisector.

If no intersections are reported then the geometric bisector consists of two analytic bisectors, i.e. of both branches of the conic. Similarly to above, the second analytic bisector is restricted to $CI(o_1) \cap CI(o_2)$.

6.4.2   Computing Bisector Intersections

Intersecting two analytic bisectors b_1 and b_2, with coordinate parameterizations (x_1, y_1) and (x_2, y_2), means to solve the following set of non-linear equations for t_1, t_2:

$$x_1(t_1) = x_2(t_2)$$

$$y_1(t_1) = y_2(t_2).$$

---

[1] Recall Definition 5.7.

Fortunately, within our algorithms, t_1 has to be equal to t_2 because both parameters constitute the offset of the same point. Hence, computing a bisector intersection is equivalent to computing a point lying at the same distance from three objects (points, lines, arcs).

For example, in the case of two bisectors defined by three circular arcs we are to solve the set of equations

$$(x(t) - xc_1)^2 + (y(t) - yc_1)^2 = (r_1 + k_1 \cdot t)^2$$

$$(x(t) - xc_2)^2 + (y(t) - yc_2)^2 = (r_2 + k_2 \cdot t)^2$$

$$(x(t) - xc_3)^2 + (y(t) - yc_3)^2 = (r_3 + k_3 \cdot t)^2$$

for t, where k_i as usual denotes the sliding direction of the circular arc c_i. Observe that $k_i^2 = 1$. By adding and subtracting these equations, $x(t)$ and $y(t)$ can be expressed as terms linear in t. After plugging these expressions into one of the above formulas, a second-degree polynomial equation in t is obtained[2]. A similar analysis applies if straight line segments are involved.

---

[2]Thanks go to Gábor Lukács, Hasse Persson, and Tamás Várady for pointing out that there is no need for iteratively searching for a solution in the case of degeneracies.

Chapter 7

The Concept of Monotonous Areas

In the sequel, we present our concept of monotonous areas within the pocket area $\mathcal{P}$. We presuppose that $\mathcal{P}$ is simply-connected and admissible, i.e. bounded by one proper contour $\mathcal{C}$. Hence, $\mathcal{C}$ is the boundary of the closure of $\mathcal{P}$ and $\mathcal{P}$ is the open area bounded by $\mathcal{C}$.

7.1   Introducing Monotonous Areas

7.1.1   Defining Monotonous Areas

Definition 7.1 (Offsetting) Let $\mathcal{A}$ be bounded by a Jordan curve $\mathcal{C}$. For $t \in \mathsf{R}_0^+$, the *offset area* $OA(\mathcal{A}, \mathcal{C}, t)$ with offset t w.r.t. $\mathcal{A}$ and $\mathcal{C}$ is given by $OA(\mathcal{A}, \mathcal{C}, t) := \{ p \in \mathcal{A} : d(p, \mathcal{C}) \geq t \}$.

We note that several different definitions of offsetting are used in practice, see Saaed *et al* [S*88b]. This variety of definitions is motivated by the various demands resulting from different applications. For instance, when offsetting polygonal objects in a solid modeler, it may be desirable to maintain the offset object within the domain of the original object (resulting in the necessity to modify the above definition).

Definition 7.2 (Innermost Point) A point $p \in \mathcal{A} \subseteq \mathcal{P}$ is called *innermost point* of $\mathcal{A}$ if $OA(\mathcal{P}, \mathcal{C}, t) \cap \mathcal{A}$ is empty for all $t > d(p, \mathcal{C})$.

Trivially, $p \in OA(\mathcal{P}, \mathcal{C}, d(p, \mathcal{C})) \cap \mathcal{A}$. Hence, innermost points of $\mathcal{P}$ can be found by continuously shrinking $\mathcal{C}$ until the offset area collapses. Observe that an innermost point is not necessarily unique: In the case of a rectangle, the set of innermost points is given by the inner bisector parallel to the legs of the rectangle.

For the sake of simplicity, in the sequel we will assume that $\mathcal{C}$ does not contain parallel straight lines and concentric circular arcs. Without this restriction, some of the following definitions and proofs would need a lot of technicalities in order to handle special cases. However, later on we will adopt a more pragmatic point of view and extend our algorithm to the general case. Dealing with the general case is particularly important for practical applications since pockets tend to have parallel lines and concentric arcs.

Definition 7.3 (Strait) For $p_1 \neq p_2 \in \mathcal{C}$, let $q := \frac{p_1 + p_2}{2}$ and $w := \frac{1}{2} d(p_1, p_2)$. Then, the points p_1, p_2 form a *strait* of $\mathcal{C}$ (and $\mathcal{P}$) with width $w > 0$ if

1. $d(q, \mathcal{C}) = w$,
2. for all $\rho > 0$, there exists $\epsilon > 0$ such that $OA(\mathcal{P}, \mathcal{C}, w + \epsilon) \cap D_i(q, \rho) \neq \emptyset$, where $i \in \{L, R\}$ and $D_L(q, \rho)$ ($D_R(q, \rho)$, respectively) denotes the half of $D(q, \rho)$ at the left-hand side (right-hand side, respectively) of (p_1, p_2).

If p_1, p_2 form a strait then the line segment (p_1, p_2) is called the *door* of the strait and q is called the *midpoint* of the strait.

Definition 7.4 (Monotonous Area) An area $\mathcal{A} \subseteq \mathcal{P}$ is called a *monotonous area* if $\mathcal{A}$

1. is an open set,

2. is (path-)connected,

3. does not intersect with any door of a strait of $\mathcal{C}$,

4. is maximal, i.e. any superset $\mathcal{A}^* \supset \mathcal{A}$ does not fulfill at least one of the conditions 1)–3).

We note that monotonous areas need not be convex: Just think of a banana-shaped pocket which does not contain straits.

Definition 7.5 (Inner Point) A point $p \in \mathcal{P}$ is called an *inner point* of $\mathcal{P}$ if p is an innermost point of a monotonous area of $\mathcal{P}$.

Thus, there exists no point within a monotonous area that has a larger clearance than the area's inner points.

7.1.2 Basic Properties of Monotonous Areas

Lemma 7.1 Doors of straits of $\mathcal{C}$ do not intersect pairwise.

Proof: Let p_1, p_2 and p_3, p_4 form straits of $\mathcal{C}$ and denote their widths by w_1 and w_2. Suppose that (p_1, p_2) and (p_3, p_4) intersect in p. Let $d_1 := d(p, p_1)$ and $d_2 := d(p, p_3)$ and denote the midpoints of the straits by q_1 and q_2. W.l.o.g. we assume that $d_1 \leq w_1$ and $d_2 \leq w_2$.
Case: Either $d_1 < w_1$ or $d_2 < w_2$. W.l.o.g. $d_1 < w_1$. By the triangle inequality and condition 1 in the definition of a strait, we get

$$w_2 \leq d(q_2, p_1) \leq d(q_2, p) + d(p, p_1) = w_2 - d_2 + d_1,$$

$$w_1 \leq d(q_1, p_3) < d(q_1, p) + d(p, p_3) = w_1 - d_1 + d_2.$$

We conclude with the contradiction $d_1 \geq d_2$ and $d_1 < d_2$.
Case: $d_1 = w_1$ and $d_2 = w_2$. By the same argument as above, we get $d_1 = d_2$. In this case, p_1, p_2, p_3, p_4 are the corners of a quadrangle Q and it is easy to see that, for any point $p_5 \in Q$, there exists $1 \leq i \leq 4$ s.t. $d(p_5, p_i) \leq w_1$. Hence, condition 2 in the definition of a strait is contradicted. $\qquad\square$

Lemma 7.2 Monotonous areas of $\mathcal{P}$ do not intersect pairwise.

Proof: Let $\mathcal{A}_1 \neq \mathcal{A}_2 \subset \mathcal{P}$ be two monotonous areas. Suppose that $\mathcal{A}_1 \cap \mathcal{A}_2 \neq \emptyset$. It is easy to see that $\mathcal{A}_1 \cup \mathcal{A}_2$ is also a monotonous area, which contradicts the maximality of $\mathcal{A}_1$ and $\mathcal{A}_2$. $\Box$

Lemma 7.3 For $p \in \mathcal{P}$, p is either contained in a monotonous area or in the door of a strait.

Proof: Suppose that p is not contained in the door of a strait. Hence, there exists $\rho > 0$ such that $D(p, \rho) \subseteq \mathcal{P}$ and $D(p, \rho)$ is not intersected by the door of a strait. Now, either the clearance disk is maximal (i.e. it is a monotonous area) or it is not maximal (i.e. it is contained in a monotonous area). In both cases, the proof is finished. $\Box$

Corollary 7.1 The pocket area $\mathcal{P}$ is partitioned into the monotonous areas and the doors of straits, i.e. members of these sets do not intersect pairwise and their union yields $\mathcal{P}$.

Corollary 7.2 A monotonous area is bounded by portions of $\mathcal{C}$ and by doors of straits.

Hence, except for the doors of straits, $\mathcal{P}$ is totally covered by the monotonous areas. The following two lemmata show that a split-up of the offset area of $\mathcal{C}$ is caused by straits of $\mathcal{C}$.

Lemma 7.4 Let $\mathcal{A}$ be a monotonous area of $\mathcal{P}$ and let w be the maximal width of straits whose doors are in the boundary of $\overline{\mathcal{A}}$. Then, $OA(\mathcal{P}, \mathcal{C}, t) \cap \overline{\mathcal{A}} \subseteq \mathcal{A}$ iff $t > w$.

Proof: If $w = 0$, then $\mathcal{A} = \mathcal{P}$ and the lemma trivially holds.
1) Hence, suppose that $w > 0$ and $OA(\mathcal{P}, \mathcal{C}, t) \cap \overline{\mathcal{A}} \subseteq \mathcal{A}$. If $t \leq w$, then $OA(\mathcal{P}, \mathcal{C}, t)$ has to intersect at least the door of that strait in the boundary of $\overline{\mathcal{A}}$ which has width w. This yields a contradiction to the supposition.
2) Suppose that $t > w$. Trivially, $OA(\mathcal{P}, \mathcal{C}, t) \cap \mathcal{C} = \emptyset$. Furthermore, $OA(\mathcal{P}, \mathcal{C}, t)$ cannot intersect the door of any strait with width $\leq w$. $\Box$

The lemma implies that a maximal connected component of $OA(\mathcal{P}, \mathcal{C}, t)$ is totally contained in $\mathcal{A}$ iff $t > w$. In other words, the task of computing the offset area of $\mathcal{C}$ can be split up into the subtasks of computing the offset area for each individual monotonous area as soon as the offset t is larger than the width of straits.

Lemma 7.5 If C has a strait with width w then there exists $\epsilon > 0$ such that $OA(\mathcal{P}, C, w + \epsilon)$ consists of at least two disjoint sets.

Proof: Let p_1, p_2 be a strait with width w. By the definition of a strait, there must exist $\epsilon > 0$ s.t. $OA(\mathcal{P}, C, w + \epsilon) \cap D_i(q, 1) \neq \emptyset$. Observe that a strait partitions $\mathcal{P}$ into two disjoint sets. Hence, since the door of the strait cannot be intersected by $OA(\mathcal{P}, C, w + \epsilon)$, this offset area consists of at least two disjoint sets.   □

Lemma 7.6 $\mathcal{VD}(C)$ is a weakly-connected, acyclic digraph[1].

Proof: Follows from the correctness of the retraction method, cf. O'Dunlaing and Yap [OY85], and Stifter [Sti88].   □

Lemma 7.7 If $OA(\mathcal{P}, C, t)$ consists of two disconnected sets, then there exists at least one strait of C with width $w < t$.

Proof: Consider $p_1 \neq p_2 \in OA(\mathcal{P}, C, t)$. Since $\mathcal{P}$ is path-connected, there exists a path between p_1 and p_2 that is completely contained in $\mathcal{P}$.

The lemma again results from the correctness of the retraction method. As described by O'Dunlaing and Yap [OY85], and Stifter [Sti88], retract p_1, p_2 onto the Voronoi diagram $\mathcal{VD}(C)$, yielding the points $p_1^V, p_2^V \in \mathcal{VD}(C)$. This retraction does not leave $OA(\mathcal{P}, C, t)$ because the clearance distance is increased. Besides, the path P composed by the retractions and a path on the Voronoi diagram between p_1^V and p_2^V has the important property that $d(P, C)$ is maximal amongst all paths totally contained in $\mathcal{P}$ that connect p_1, p_2.

Case 1: $d(P, C) \geq t$. Then, $P \subseteq OA(\mathcal{P}, C, t)$. If every pair of points of $OA(\mathcal{P}, C, t)$ can be connected by a path P with $d(P, C) \geq t$, then the offset area is path-connected. Contradiction!

Case 2: $d(P, C) < t$. Let $q \in P$ such that $d(q, C) = d(P, C)$ and let $a_1 \neq a_2 \in C$ such that $d(p, a_1) = d(p, a_2) = d(P, C)$. Since, P has maximal $d(P, C)$, such a pair a_1, a_2 must exist. We will now prove that a_1, a_2 form a strait with width $d(P, C)$. Assume that there exists $\rho > 0$ such that for all $q' \in D(q, \rho) \cap P$, $d(q', C) = d(P, C)$. A case analysis shows that this can only happen if C contains parallel lines or concentric arcs. Thus, a_1, a_2 form a strait of C with width $d(P, C) < t$.   □

Theorem 7.1 Let $\mathcal{A} \subseteq \mathcal{P}$ be a monotonous area. Then, for all $t > 0$, the set $\mathcal{A} \cap OA(\mathcal{P}, C, t)$ is path-connected or empty.

---

[1]The orientation of the Voronoi edges is explained on Page 94.

Proof: The proof follows from the preceding lemma. □

Corollary 7.3 The set $OA(\mathcal{P}, \mathcal{C}, t)$ is path-connected or empty for all $t \geq 0$ iff $\mathcal{P}$ consists of one monotonous area.

7.2   Determining Monotonous Areas

7.2.1   Monotonous Areas and Voronoi Diagrams

The following lemmata establish important relations between the monotonous areas of $\mathcal{P}$ and the Voronoi diagram $\mathcal{VD}(\mathcal{C})$. These relations will be exploited when stating a simple algorithm for obtaining the monotonous areas of $\mathcal{P}$.

Recall from Page 91 that the contour clearance monotonously increases when moving along an edge $e \in \mathcal{VD}(\mathcal{C})$ from its tail to its head. If the defining objects of e are no parallel line segments and no concentric arcs, a simple case analysis shows that the clearance is even strictly monotonously increasing.

Lemma 7.8 Every innermost point of $\mathcal{P}$ is a node of $\mathcal{VD}(\mathcal{C})$.

Proof: Let p be an innermost point of $\mathcal{P}$.
1) Suppose that $p \in \mathcal{VA}(o, \mathcal{C})$ for some $o \in \mathcal{C}$ and denote the clearance line of p w.r.t. o by ℓ. Then, rectract p along ℓ onto $\mathcal{VP}(o, \mathcal{C})$ yielding the point $p' \in \mathcal{VP}(o, \mathcal{C})$. Obviously, $d(p, \mathcal{C}) < d(p', \mathcal{C})$. Hence, every innermost point must lie on $\mathcal{VD}(\mathcal{C})$.
2) Now, suppose that $p \in e \in \mathcal{VD}(\mathcal{C})$, but p is not an endpoint of e. By the remark stated above, the clearance of the head of e is larger than the clearance of p (and the head of e lies in $\mathcal{P}$). Thus, we conclude that $p \in N(\mathcal{VD}(\mathcal{C}))$. □

Corollary 7.4 Every inner point of $\mathcal{P}$ is a Voronoi node that has no outgoing edges.

Lemma 7.9 Every node $v \in N(\mathcal{VD}(\mathcal{C}))$ has at most two outgoing edges.

Proof: Let e be an outgoing edge of v and denote the defining contour object at the left-hand side (right-hand side, respectively) of the oriented edge e by o_L (by o_R, respectively). Let $p_L \in o_L$ and $p_R \in o_R$ be such that $d(o_L, o_R) = d(p_L, p_R)$. Suppose that an outgoing edge of v intersects $\triangle(v, p_L, p_R)$. Then, by the triangle inequality, $d(v, p_L) \leq d(q, p_L)$, and equality only holds if $v = p$. Suppose that the node v has a second outgoing edge e'.
Case 1: e' lies at the left-hand side of the oriented polygon $p_L \rightarrow v \rightarrow p_R$.

W.l.o.g. assume that e' lies at the right-hand side of e. Denote the left defining object of e' by $o' \in \mathcal{C}$ and let $p' \in o'$ such that $d(v, o') = d(v, p')$. Obviously, $d(v, p') = d(v, p_L)$. Since (v, p') does not intersect e, e is at least partially contained in the cone bounded by the line segments (v, p_L) and (v, p'). By the triangle inequality, there exists $q \in e$ such that $d(q, p') < d(v, p')$, which yields a contradiction.

Case 2: e' lies at the right-hand side of (p_L, p_R). Recall that in this case v necessarily must be the midpoint of p_L and p_R. Similarly to Case 1, no other outgoing edge of v can lie on the same side, which completes the proof. $\square$

Lemma 7.10 Every node $v \in N(\mathcal{VD}(\mathcal{C}))$ that has exactly two outgoing edges is the midpoint of a strait.

Proof: Similar to the preceding proof. $\square$

Lemma 7.11 Every monotonous area contains at least one inner point.

Lemma 7.12 Every node $v \in N(\mathcal{VD}(\mathcal{C}))$ that has no outgoing edges is an inner point.

Proof: Suppose that v has no outgoing edges but is no inner point. Obviously, p cannot be contained in the door of a strait. Let $\mathcal{A}$ be the monotonous area containing p and denote the inner point of $\mathcal{A}$ by q. Let $P \subset \mathcal{VD}(\mathcal{C})$ be the path connecting p and q. Since p, q have only incoming edges and P is incident upon p, q, P must contain a node that has two outgoing edges. Thus, P passes through a strait, yielding a contradiction to $p, q \in \mathcal{A}$. $\square$

Corollary 7.5 Every monotonous area contains exactly one inner point.

Summarizing, we can state the following Characterization Theorem that allows us to algorithmically determine the straits and inner points, i.e. the monotonous areas of $\mathcal{P}$.

Theorem 7.2 (Characterization Theorem) 1) Inner points of $\mathcal{P}$ are exactly those node of $\mathcal{VD}(\mathcal{C})$ which have no outgoing edges. 2) Midpoints of straits are exactly those nodes of $\mathcal{VD}(\mathcal{C})$ which have two disjoint outgoing edges.

7.2.2   Algorithm for Determining Monotonous Areas

In the preceding subsection, we have established a characterization of inner points and midpoints of straits by means of the Voronoi diagram. This characterization enables us to state the following algorithm for computing monotonous areas.

As stated in Table 7.1, the algorithm Monotonous_Area is called with an arbitrary contour bisector used as a start edge. The algorithm first searches for an inner point by means of the algorithm Inner_Point. Then, Straits detects the straits that bound the monotonous area containing the determined inner point. Since each strait corresponds to exactly two monotonous areas, for each strait, Monotonous_Area is recursively called in order to determine the other monotonous area bounded by this strait. Of course, inner points and midpoints of straits are not dealt with as single points. Rather, incident edges of the Voronoi diagram constitute the input and output parameters.

Algorithm Monotonous_Area ($\downarrow$ *Start_Edge*):
Begin
      Inner_Point ($\downarrow$ *Start_Edge*, $\uparrow$ *Incident_Edge*)
      Straits ($\downarrow$ *Incident_Edge*, $\uparrow$ *Set_of_Edges*)
      Build monotonous area using *Incident_Edge, Set_of_Edges*
      while *Set_of_Edges* $\neq \emptyset$ **do**
        Pick (*Edge$_1$, Edge$_2$*) $\in$ *Set_of_Edges*
        if *Edge$_1$* $\neq$ *Start_Edge* **then**
          Monotonous_Area ($\downarrow$ *Edge$_2$*)
        end_if
        Set_of_Edges := *Set_of_Edges* \ {(*Edge$_1$, Edge$_2$*)}
      end_while
End Monotonous_Area.

Table 7.1: Algorithm Monotonous_Area.

Algorithm Inner_Point determines an inner point by searching along the edges of the Voronoi diagram, cf. Table 7.2. Merely, the algorithm examines the head of *Edge$_1$* and searches for an outgoing edge. Clearly, an outgoing edge is characterized by a larger upper bound on the parameter interval. An inner point is guaranteed to be found because the contour clearance is strictly monotonously increasing during the search. Besides, the inner point is contained in the same monotonous area that contains the start edge.

Algorithm Straits is called in order to search for the midpoints of straits, cf. Table 7.3. The input parameter passed to Strait contains a pointer to an edge incident upon the actual area's inner point. By CCW examining the incoming

Algorithm Inner_Point ($\downarrow$ *Start_Edge*, $\uparrow$ *Incident_Edge*):
Begin
    $Edge_1 := Start\_Edge$
    $Edge_2 := Edge_1\uparrow.Head\_CCW$
    repeat
      if $Edge_1\uparrow.Upper\_Bound < Edge_2\uparrow.Upper\_Bound$ **then**
        $Edge_1 := Edge_2$
        $Edge_2 := Edge_1\uparrow.Head\_CCW$
      else
        $Edge_2 := Edge_2\uparrow.Head\_CCW$
      end_if
    until $Edge_1 = Edge_2$
    $Incident\_Edge := Edge_1$
End Inner_Point.

Table 7.2: Algorithm Inner_Point.

Algorithm Straits ($\downarrow$ *Incident_Edge*, $\uparrow$ *Set_of_Edges*):
Begin
    $Set\_of\_Edges := \emptyset$
    $Edge_1 := Incident\_Edge$
    repeat
      if $\neg\ Edge_1\uparrow.contour\_bisector$ **then**
        Find_Strait ($\downarrow Edge_1$, $\updownarrow Set\_of\_Edges$)
      end_if
      $Edge_1 := Edge_1\uparrow.Head\_CCW$
    until $Edge_1 = Incident\_Edge$
End Straits.

Table 7.3: Algorithm Straits.

edges of the inner point, the recursive algorithm Find_Strait is called for each
incoming edge that is no contour bisector. Find_Strait checks whether there exists
an outgoing edge incident upon the tail of its start edge, cf. Table 7.4. In this
case, a strait has been found and Set_of_Straits is updated. Otherwise, a recursive
call is made for each incoming edge incident in the tail of the start edge.

Algorithm Find_Strait ($\downarrow$ *Start_Edge*, $\updownarrow$ *Set_of_Edges*):
Begin
      $Edge_1 := Start\_Edge$
      $Edge_2 := Edge_1\uparrow.Tail\_CCW$
      while $Edge_1\uparrow.Lower\_Bound \neq Edge_2\uparrow.Lower\_Bound$ **do**
        if $\neg$ $Edge_2\uparrow.contour\_bisector$ **then**
          Find_Strait ($\downarrow$ $Edge_2$, $\updownarrow$ *Set_of_Edges*)
        end_if
        $Edge_2 := Edge_2\uparrow.Head\_CCW$
      end_while
      if $Edge_1 \neq Edge_2$ **then**
        $Set\_of\_Edges := Set\_of\_Edges \cup \{(Edge_1, Edge_2)\}$
      end_if
End Find_Strait.

Table 7.4: Algorithm Find_Strait.

7.3   Implementational Issues

7.3.1   Representing Monotonous Areas

Algorithm Monotonous_Area starts in a monotonous area of $\mathcal{P}$ and, for each further call, establishes the information on straits and inner points for the monotonous area entered at the start bisector *Start_Bisector*. Hence, the processing order of the monotonous areas is reflected by a rooted tree, whose root corresponds to the first monotonous area that is processed and where area $\mathcal{A}_1$ is a father of area $\mathcal{A}_2$ if $\mathcal{A}_1$ and $\mathcal{A}_2$ share a strait and if $\mathcal{A}_2$ is entered from $\mathcal{A}_1$ via this strait.

In our application, it turned out to be convenient that the root of the tree of monotonous areas corresponds to an area whose inner point is an innermost point of $\mathcal{P}$. Trivially, such an appropriate starting area can be found in linear time by a simple scan of the parameter upper bounds of the edges of $\mathcal{VD}(\mathcal{C})$.

In addition, the algorithm Straits determines the straits of a monotonous area in a specific manner such that they are arranged in CCW order around the area's inner point. Hence, it is obvious to represent the topological relations between monotonous areas by a rooted tree, whose edges correspond to edges of the Voronoi diagram that are incident upon the midpoints of straits between monotonous areas. Additionally, the straits are maintained in (doubly-)linked lists. The corresponding data types *Area* and *Strait* are given by Table 7.5 and Table 7.6.

type *Area_Ptr* = **pointer to** *Area*
type *Strait_Ptr* = **pointer to** *Strait*

type *Area* =
   record
     Inner_Point: Point
     Incident_Edge: Edge_Ptr
     Straits: Strait_Ptr
   end_record

Table 7.5: Data Type *Area*.

type *Strait* =
   record
     Mid_Point: Point
     $Edge_1$, $Edge_2$: *Edge_Ptr*
     $Area_1$, $Area_2$: *Area_Ptr*
     $Next\_Strait_1$, $Next\_Strait_2$: *Strait_Ptr*
   end_record

Table 7.6: Data Type *Strait*.

7.3.2 Handling Parallel Lines and Concentric Arcs

In the case of parallel straight line segments or concentric circular arcs, it is not guaranteed that all analytic bisectors have a strictly monotonously increasing contour clearance. In more detail, if two parallel line segments or two concentric arcs define a bisector, then this bisector has constant contour clearance. Hence, no straightforward scheme is apparent for orientating such edges of the Voronoi diagram. However, our algorithm for determining monotonous areas heavily relies on the fact that all edges are oriented in a way such that they are pointing towards the inner points.

Besides, a strait needs not longer be a pair of points. Rather, 'parallel' corridors of equal width bounded by parallel lines and concentric arcs may constitute bottle-necks of C. As a consequence, condition 2 in the definition of a strait may no longer be satisfied. Hence, a more detailed classification would be needed.

We have contented ourselves to guaranteeing the correctness of Corollary 7.1, Lemma 7.4, and Theorem 7.1. This goal can be achieved by means of the following pragmatic approach[2]:

---
[2] Clearly, this concept could also be formalized.

1. For every bisector b defined by parallel lines or concentric arcs, pick out a point $p \in \underline{b}$ and split b at p into two edges pointing towards p. This radical way of simply imposing an orientation abolishes unoriented edges.

2. Run the algorithm Monotonous_Area as described above. It yields a subdivision of $\mathcal{P}$ into 'monotonous areas' bounded by 'straits'.

3. Starting at the root of the tree of monotonous areas, scan the tree and eliminate those monotonous areas that merely consist of the above mentioned parallel corridors. In more detail, an area is eliminated if the clearance of its inner point is equal to the minimal width of its straits. If $\mathcal{A}_2$ is such an area and $\mathcal{A}_2$ is a son of $\mathcal{A}_1$, then $\mathcal{A}_2$ is adjoined to $\mathcal{A}_1$. Additionally, the strait between $\mathcal{A}_1$ and $\mathcal{A}_2$ is eliminated.

This simple approach guarantees that the main properties of monotonous areas are preserved even within the more general setting. For the sequel, when speaking about monotonous areas, we mean the areas resulting from the partition of $\mathcal{P}$ established by this algorithm.

Chapter 8

Generating the Tool Path

In this chapter, we use the introduced geometric concepts for efficiently generating the offset tool path. The task of generating the offset tool path is mainly subdivided into two subtasks: the determination of suitable offsets, i.e. pass distances, and the construction of offset curves corresponding to these offsets.

8.1 Optimal Pass Distance

Restricting to a monotonous area, in this section we investigate the following problem:

Given: an 'inner' cutter pass with offset t_2,

Determine: the offset $t_1 < t_2$ of an 'outer' cutter pass s.t. nothing is left uncut between these two cutter passes.

8.1.1 Basic Definitions

Recall from the last chapter on monotonous areas that the offset area $OA(\mathcal{A}, C, t)$ of a simply-connected and path-connected area $\mathcal{A}$ bounded by a Jordan curve C is the set of points of $\mathcal{A}$ whose clearance is not less than t. However, when dealing with offset cutter paths we are more interested in the boundaries of offset areas.

Definition 8.1 (Offset Curve) For an offset $t \in \mathsf{R}_0^+$, the *(set of) offset curves* $OC(\mathcal{P}, C, t)$ w.r.t. t, $\mathcal{P}$, and C is given by $OC(\mathcal{P}, C, t) := \{p \in \overline{\mathcal{P}} : d(p, C) = t\}$.

By making use of the Voronoi diagram, we similarly identify the components of offset curves.

Definition 8.2 (Offset Object) For $o \in C$ and $t \in \mathsf{R}_0^+$, the *(set of) offset objects* $OO(\mathcal{P}, C, t, o)$ of o with offset t w.r.t. $\mathcal{P}$ and C is given by $OO(\mathcal{P}, C, t, o) := OC(\mathcal{P}, C, t) \cap \mathcal{VA}(o, C)$.

Obviously, $OC(\mathcal{P}, C, t) = \cup_{o \in C} OO(\mathcal{P}, C, t, o)$. In the sequel, we will repeatedly identify that portion of $\mathcal{P}$ which is machined by a tool moving along a curve.

Definition 8.3 Let C be a curve and let ρ denote the radius of a cutter circle. Then, the area $TS(C, \rho)$ defined by the *tool* with radius ρ *swept* along C is given by $TS(C, \rho) := \bigcup_{p \in C} D(p, \rho)$.

For shorthand, for an offset curve $OC(\mathcal{P}, C, t)$ and a monotonous area $\mathcal{A}$, we let

$$\partial TS(OC(\mathcal{P}, C, t), \rho)_{\mathcal{A}} := \mathcal{A} \cap [\partial TS(OC(\mathcal{P}, C, t), \rho) \setminus OA(\mathcal{P}, C, t)],$$

i.e. $\partial TS(OC(\mathcal{P}, \mathcal{C}, t), \rho)_{\mathcal{A}}$ is the outwards boundary (restricted to $\mathcal{A}$) of the area defined by the tool with radius ρ swept along the offset curve $OC(\mathcal{P}, \mathcal{C}, t)$.

Definition 8.4 (Optimal Pass Distance) Let $\mathcal{A} \subseteq \mathcal{P}$ and let ρ_1, ρ_2 denote the radii of two cutters. For two offsets $t_1 < t_2$, *nothing is left uncut* between $C_1 := OC(\mathcal{P}, \mathcal{C}, t_1) \cap \mathcal{A}$ and $C_2 := OC(\mathcal{P}, \mathcal{C}, t_2) \cap \mathcal{A}$ w.r.t. ρ_1, ρ_2 if

$$TS(C_1, \rho_1) \cup TS(C_2, \rho_2) \supseteq \mathcal{A} \cap [OA(\mathcal{P}, \mathcal{C}, t_1) \setminus OA(\mathcal{P}, \mathcal{C}, t_2)].$$

The cutter *pass distance* $d(t_1, t_2) := t_2 - t_1$ is called *optimal* w.r.t. $\mathcal{A}$ and ρ_1, ρ_2 if, for all $t_0 < t_1$, the above condition does no longer hold with t_0 substituted for t_1.

Hence, the cutter pass distance is optimal if nothing is left uncut between two neighbouring passes (within a monotonous area) and if the pass distance cannot be chosen larger in order to meet this goal. As stated in the survey chapter on contour-parallel milling, we would like to emphasize again that cutter pass distances have to obey to some further technological restrictions in order to be really optimal.

8.1.2 Characterization of an Optimal Pass Distance

For this subsection, we assume that $\mathcal{A}$ is a monotonous area. The following lemma on the lower and upper bound of an optimal pass distance is straightforward.

Lemma 8.1 If $d(t_1, t_2)$ is an optimal pass distance with respect to $\mathcal{A} \subseteq \mathcal{P}$ and ρ_1, ρ_2, then $\rho_1 \leq d(t_1, t_2) \leq \rho_1 + \rho_2$.

Definition 8.5 A curve $C \subseteq \partial TS(OC(\mathcal{P}, \mathcal{C}, t), \rho)_{\mathcal{A}}$ is called *critical* if there exists a point $c \in \mathcal{VD}(C) \cap OC(\mathcal{P}, \mathcal{C}, t)$ such that $C \subseteq \mathcal{C}(c, \rho)$.

Hence, critical curves are formed by portions of the cutter circle centered at endpoints of offset objects.

Lemma 8.2 For $t \in \mathbb{R}_0^+$ and $0 < \rho < t$, $\partial TS(OC(\mathcal{P}, \mathcal{C}, t), \rho)_{\mathcal{A}}$ consists of portions of $OC(\mathcal{P}, \mathcal{C}, t - \rho)$ and of critical curves.

Proof: Since $OC(\mathcal{P}, \mathcal{C}, t) = \cup_{o \in \mathcal{C}} OO(\mathcal{P}, \mathcal{C}, t, o)$, the proof can be carried out by a simple case analysis. $\qquad \Box$

Lemma 8.3 For $p \in \mathcal{A} \setminus [OA(\mathcal{P}, \mathcal{C}, t) \cup TS(OC(\mathcal{P}, \mathcal{C}, t), \rho)]$, $d(p, \mathcal{C}) \leq \max\{d(q, \mathcal{C}) : q \in \partial TS(OC(\mathcal{P}, \mathcal{C}, t), \rho)_{\mathcal{A}}\}$.

Proof: Suppose that $d(p,\mathcal{C}) > \max\{d(q,\mathcal{C}) : q \in \partial TS(OC(\mathcal{P},\mathcal{C},t),\rho)_{\mathcal{A}}\}$. Let $q \in \mathcal{A} \cap [OA(\mathcal{P},\mathcal{C},t) \cup TS(OC(\mathcal{P},\mathcal{C},t),\rho)]$ s.t. $d(q,\mathcal{C}) = d(p,\mathcal{C})$. Since $\mathcal{A}$ is a monotonous area, $OA(\mathcal{P},\mathcal{C},d(p,\mathcal{C}))$ is path-connected. However, any path connecting p and q must cross $\partial TS(OC(\mathcal{P},\mathcal{C},t),\rho)_{\mathcal{A}}$, yielding a contradiction. $\square$

Corollary 8.1 Let $d := \max\{d(q,\mathcal{C}) : q \in \partial TS(OC(\mathcal{P},\mathcal{C},t_2),\rho_2)_{\mathcal{A}}\}$. If $d \leq t_1 + \rho_1$ then nothing is left uncut between $OC(\mathcal{P},\mathcal{C},t_1) \cap \mathcal{A}$ and $OC(\mathcal{P},\mathcal{C},t_2) \cap \mathcal{A}$ w.r.t. ρ_1, ρ_2.

Lemma 8.4 Let $p \in \partial TS(OC(\mathcal{P},\mathcal{C},t),\rho)_{\mathcal{A}}$. If $d(p,\mathcal{C}) > t - \rho$ then a critical curve C exists s.t. $p \in C$.

Proof: Observe that for all $C \subseteq \partial TS(OC(\mathcal{P},\mathcal{C},t),\rho)_{\mathcal{A}}$, if C does not contain a critical curve then $t - \rho = \min\{d(q,\mathcal{C}) : q \in C\} = \max\{d(q,\mathcal{C}) : q \in C\}$, which establishes the claim. $\square$

Lemma 8.5 Let $C \subseteq \partial TS(OC(\mathcal{P},\mathcal{C},t),\rho)_{\mathcal{A}}$ be a critical curve and let $p \in \overline{C}$ s.t. $d(p,\mathcal{C}) = \max\{d(q,\mathcal{C}) : q \in \overline{C}\}$. If $p \notin \mathcal{VD}(C)$ then there exists $o \in C$ s.t.

1. o is a CCW arc,

2. $p \in \mathcal{VA}(o,C)$, and

3. $d(p,o) = \max\{d(q,o) : q \in \overline{C}\}$.

Proof: Denote the non-empty restriction of C to $\mathcal{VA}(o,C)$ by C_o. A simple case analysis shows that $p \notin C_o$ except if the conditions 1–3 of above are fulfilled. $\square$

By convention, we call such a p a *critical point*.

8.2 Computing Optimal Offsets

8.2.1 Algorithmical Characterization

We summarize our results in the following theorem which refers to Algorithm Critical_Point stated in Table 8.1. The proof of the theorem follows immediately from the preceding lemmata. The algorithm's input parameter *Set_of_Curves* corresponds to the set of maximal critical curves of $\partial TS(OC(\mathcal{P},\mathcal{C},t_2))_{\mathcal{A}}$.

Theorem 8.1 Let $\mathcal{A} \subseteq \mathcal{P}$ be a monotonous area and let ρ_1, ρ_2 denote the radii of two cutters. For two offsets $t_1 < t_2$, nothing is left uncut between $C_1 :=$

Algorithm Critical_Point($\downarrow$ *Set_of_Curves*, $\uparrow$ *Critical_Point*):
Begin

    Set_of_Critical_Curves := *Set_of_Curves*

    Set_of_Critical_Points := $\emptyset$

    while *Set_of_Critical_Curves* $\neq \emptyset$ **do**

      Pick $C \in$ *Set_of_Critical_Curves*

      Set_of_Critical_Points := $(\mathcal{VD}(C) \cap C) \cup$ *Set_of_Critical_Points*

      for $s \in C$ **do**

        if s is a CCW arc and $C_s := \mathcal{VA}(s, C) \cap C \neq \emptyset$ **then**

          Let $p \in C_s$ s.t. $d(p, s) = \max \{d(q, s) : q \in C_s\}$

          Set_of_Critical_Points := $\{p\} \cup$ *Set_of_Critical_Points*

        end_if

      end_for

      Set_of_Critical_Curves := *Set_of_Critical_Curves* $\setminus \{C\}$

    end_while

    Let $p \in$ *Set_of_Critical_Points* s.t.

      $d(p, C) = \max \{d(q, C) : q \in$ *Set_of_Critical_Points*$\}$

    Critical_Point := p

End Critical_Point.

Table 8.1: Algorithm Critical_Point.

$OC(\mathcal{P}, \mathcal{C}, t_1) \cap \mathcal{A}$ and $C_2 := OC(\mathcal{P}, \mathcal{C}, t_2) \cap \mathcal{A}$ w.r.t. ρ_1, ρ_2 iff the critical point p determined by Algorithm Critical_Point is contained in $\mathcal{TS}(OC(\mathcal{P}, \mathcal{C}, t_1) \cap \mathcal{A}$. Similarly, the cutter pass distance $d(t_1, t_2) = t_2 - t_1$ is optimal w.r.t. $\mathcal{A}$ and ρ_1, ρ_2 iff $t_1 = d(p, C) - \rho_1$.

Of course, in our implementation GEOPOCKET we have refined Critical_Point and have avoided to intersect a critical curve C with all edges of $\mathcal{VD}(C)$. Rather, it is sufficient to intersect C with those edges of the actual monotonous area that point towards the center of C. Similarly, only those Voronoi areas have to be tested whose Voronoi polygons are intersected by C.

Up to now, we have been concerned with computing optimal pass distances with respect to individual monotonous areas. However, cutter passes may enter several monotonous areas. Hence, we have to worry about optimal offsets rather than about optimal pass distances.

Let $\mathcal{A}^t$ denote the set of monotonous areas of $\mathcal{P}$ which are entered by $OC(\mathcal{P}, \mathcal{C}, t)$. Then, we define the meaning of optimal offsets.

Definition 8.6 (Optimal Offsets) For $t \in \mathbb{R}_0^+$, let $\{\mathcal{A}_1, \ldots, \mathcal{A}_j\} := \mathcal{A}^t$ and associate an offset $t_i > t$ with each $\mathcal{A}_i$. Then, the offsets $t, t_1, \ldots, t_j$ are *optimal* w.r.t. ρ_1, ρ_2 if

1. for $1 \le i \le j$, nothing is left uncut between $OC(\mathcal{P}, \mathcal{C}, t) \cap \mathcal{A}_i$ and $OC(\mathcal{P}, \mathcal{C}, t_i) \cap \mathcal{A}_i$ w.r.t. ρ_1, ρ_2,

2. for $1 \le i \le j$, $t_i = t_{i'}$ if $\mathcal{A}_{i'} \in \mathcal{A}^{t_i}$,

3. conditions 1 and 2 are no longer fulfilled after enlarging one or more t_i.

8.2.2 Algorithm

In our practical implementation GEOPOCKET the scheme presented above for computing optimal pass distances has been inverted; i.e. for a given outer pass, the offset of the next inner pass is determined. This inverted scheme is conceptually not different from the original scheme but is a bit more complicated to describe. However, a properly modified version of the last theorem is also valid for the inverted scheme. The main advantage of the inverted scheme is that optimal offsets can easily be computed from optimal pass distances.

We begin with the outmost cutter pass and determine the optimal offsets of the next inner passes. In the algorithm Offsets, cf. Table 8.2, optimal pass distances are separately computed for every monotonous area by means of Next_Offset, which relies on the previously discussed algorithm Critical_Point.

Then, starting at that monotonous area $\mathcal{A}$ which has a minimal offset t associated with, those monotonous areas of $\mathcal{A}^t$ are determined by means of the recursive algorithm Neighbours, cf. Table 8.3, which intersect the maximal connected component of $OC(\mathcal{P}, \mathcal{C}, t)$ that is intersected by $\mathcal{A}$. This task envolves checking whether two monotonous areas are separated by a strait with width $\ge t$. For all monotonous areas that intersect this connected component, the previously computed offset is reduced to t. Besides, all these areas are flagged. Then, the same process is performed for that monotonous area which has a minimal offset associated with (among the still unflagged areas). In this way, optimal offsets are determined from the precomputed optimal pass distances.

If the maximal connected component of $OA(\mathcal{P}, \mathcal{C}, t)$ that intersects $\mathcal{A}$ is completely contained in $\mathcal{A}$, i.e. Neighbours reports no other monotonous areas, then t is greater than the widths of doors of straits corresponding to $\mathcal{A}$. Hence, the offset calculation for $\mathcal{A}$ can be finished without taking care of the other monotonous areas. The corresponding algorithm Finish is straightforward.

By repeatedly applying this scheme, the algorithm Offsets determines optimal offsets for all cutter passes. In the algorithms, we presume the procedures Push and Pop operating on stacks and the procedures First, Next, Delete, and Sort

Algorithm Offsets($\uparrow$ *Offset_Stack*):
Begin
    Area := First($\downarrow$ *List_of_Areas*, $\uparrow$ *end_of_list*)
    while $\neg$ *end_of_list* **do**
      while $\neg$ *end_of_list* **do**
        area_flag[Area] := **false**
        Next_Offset($\downarrow$ *Area*, $\uparrow$ *Offset*)
        Area := Next($\downarrow$ *List_of_Areas*, $\downarrow$ *Area*, $\uparrow$ *end_of_list*)
      end_while
      Sort($\updownarrow$ *List_of_Areas*, $\downarrow$ *Offset*)
      Area := First($\downarrow$ *List_of_Areas*, $\uparrow$ *end_of_list*)
      while $\neg$ *end_of_list* **do**
        if $\neg$ *area_flag*[*Area*] **then**
          area_flag[*Area*] := **true**
          Push($\updownarrow$ *Offset_Stack*[*Area*], $\downarrow$ *Offset*[*Area*])
          Neighbours($\downarrow$ *Area*, $\downarrow$ *Offset*, $\updownarrow$ *Offset_Stack*, $\updownarrow$ *area_flag*,
                     $\uparrow$ *end_flag*)
          if *end_flag* **then**
            Finish($\downarrow$ *Area*, $\updownarrow$ *Offset_Stack*)
            Delete($\updownarrow$ *List_of_Areas*, $\downarrow$ *Area*)
          end_if
        end_if
        Area := Next($\downarrow$ *List_of_Areas*, $\downarrow$ *Area*, $\uparrow$ *end_of_list*)
      end_while
      Area := First($\downarrow$ *List_of_Areas*, $\uparrow$ *end_of_list*)
    end_while
End Offsets.

Table 8.2: Algorithm Offsets.

operating on lists (and doing the jobs indicated by their names). For a monotonous area $\mathcal{A}$, the computed pass offsets are stored in the stack *Offset_Stack*[$\mathcal{A}$]. Besides, *List_of_Areas* is a list initially containing all monotonous areas of $\mathcal{P}$.

Algorithm Neighbours($\downarrow$ *Area*, $\downarrow$ *Offset*, $\updownarrow$ *Offset_Stack*, $\updownarrow$ *area_flag*, $\uparrow$ *end_flag*)
Begin
  List_of_Neighbours := list of monotonous areas sharing a strait
   with width $\geq$ *Offset* with *Area*
  New_Area := First($\downarrow$ *List_of_Neighbours*, $\uparrow$ *end_of_list*)
  if $\neg$ *end_of_list* **then**
   repeat
    if $\neg$ *area_flag*[*New_Area*] **then**
     area_flag[*New_Area*] := **true**
     Push($\updownarrow$ *Offset_Stack*[*New_Area*], $\downarrow$ *Offset*[*Area*])
     Neighbours($\downarrow$ *New_Area*, $\downarrow$ *Offset*, $\updownarrow$ *Offset_Stack*, $\updownarrow$ *area_flag*,
         $\uparrow$ *end_flag*)
    end_if
    Area := Next($\downarrow$ *List_of_Neighbours*, $\downarrow$ *Area*, $\uparrow$ *end_of_list*)
   until *end_of_list*
   end_flag := **false**
  else
   end_flag := **true**
  end_if
End Neighbours.

Table 8.3: Algorithm Neighbours.

8.3   Tool Path Assembly

8.3.1   Algorithm

Given the pass offsets for every individual monotonous area, generating the tool path $\mathcal{TP}$ merely means

1. computing (portions of) offset curves at given offsets,

2. threading up these curves in order to obtain a continuous tool path,

We start with generating offset curves. We presuppose that, for every inner point, its clearance line segment has been inserted as a new edge of the Voronoi diagram $\mathcal{VD}(\mathcal{C})$ (after properly subdividing a boundary object). Besides, we assume that with every edge $e \in \mathcal{VD}(\mathcal{C})$ a boolean value *incident* is associated with, indicating whether e is such a 'special' edge. Furthermore, we assume that the doors of straits have been inserted as 'normal' Voronoi edges[1].

---

[1]This assumption considerably facilitates the description of the algorithm Offset_Object.

The following algorithm Cutter_Pass computes that portion C of the offset curve $OC(\mathcal{P}, \mathcal{C}, t)$ which starts at the intersection between the special edge $Edge_1$ and $OC(\mathcal{P}, \mathcal{C}, t)$, and which ends when the next CCW intersection of $OC(\mathcal{P}, \mathcal{C}, t)$ with a special edge $Edge_2$ is encountered, cf. Table 8.4.

Algorithm Cutter_Pass($\downarrow$ $Edge_1$, $\downarrow$ t, $\uparrow$ C, $\uparrow$ $Edge_2$):
Begin
    $C := \emptyset$
    $Edge_3 := Edge_1$
    repeat
      Offset_Object($\downarrow$ $Edge_3$, $\downarrow$ t, $\uparrow$ $Edge_2$)
      $Object := Edge_3\uparrow.R\_Face$
      Adjoin the offset object of $Object$ (between $Edge_3$ and $Edge_2$) to C
      $Edge_3 := Edge_2$
    until $Edge_3\uparrow.incident$
End Cutter_Pass.

Table 8.4: Algorithm Cutter_Pass.

Obviously, the endpoint of one offset object is the startpoint of the succeeding offset object. The Voronoi edges containing these endpoints are determined by means of the algorithm Offset_Object, cf. Table 8.5. Offset_Object merely performs a CCW scan of the Voronoi polygon of the right defining object of the oriented edge $Edge_1$.

What remains to do is to assemble the single passes in order to generate the whole tool path. This task is executed by algorithm Tool_Path, cf. Table 8.6. Starting at the inner point of a monotonous $Area$, the tool path $\mathcal{TP}$ is generated by computing cutter passes by means of the algorithm Cutter_Pass, and by stepping outwards between neighbouring passes (in the straightforward algorithm Machine_Outwards). This process continues until the pass offset is less than a specified clearance $Margin$. If another monotonous area New_Area is entered by the tool during this process, Tool_Path is recursively called for generating the tool path for the 'inner part' of New_Area until the 'old' offset $Offset[Area]$ is reached.

In addition, the *machined_flag* of every entered monotonous area is set to true. Hence, scanning the areas after the first termination of the algorithm Tool_Path reveals whether all areas have been entered. If there exists a monotonous area $\mathcal{A}$ that has not at all been entered, Tool_Path has to be called for a second time in order to machine $\mathcal{A}$. In this case, $\mathcal{A}$ is separated from the previously machined monotonous areas by a strait whose width is less than the required offset of the

Algorithm Offset_Object($\downarrow$ $Edge_1$, $\downarrow t$, $\uparrow$ $Edge_2$):
Begin
    $Edge_3 := Edge_1$
    $Edge_2 := Edge_3\uparrow.Head\_CCW$
    while $Edge_3\uparrow.Upper\_Bound < Edge_2\uparrow.Upper\_Bound$ **do**
      $Edge_3 := Edge_2$
      $Edge_2 := Edge_3\uparrow.Head\_CCW$
    end_while
    while $Edge_2\uparrow.Lower\_Bound > t$ **do**
      $Edge_3 := Edge_2$
      $Edge_2 := Edge_3\uparrow.Tail\_CCW$
    end_while
End Offset_Object.

Table 8.5: Algorithm Offset_Object.

outmost cutter pass. Thus, the tool cannot pass through this strait and a tool retraction cannot be avoided.

We would like to remark that algorithm Tool_Path needs no amendments in order to generate the tool path thereby using two different-sized tools: First, Tool_Path is called with a suitably large *Margin* in order to prevent machining those regions intended to be cut by the second tool. In a second pass, Tool_Path is again called for the same monotonous area, now determining the tool path for the second tool.

8.3.2   Correctness

Definition 8.7 (Machinable Area) For a pocket $\mathcal{P}$ (with boundary $\mathcal{C}$), a cutter radius ρ and a margin width $\epsilon \geq 0$, the *machinable area* $\mathcal{MA}$ of $\mathcal{P}$ w.r.t. ρ and ϵ is defined as $\mathcal{MA}(\mathcal{P}, \rho, \epsilon) := \cup_{p \in \mathcal{P}} \{D(p, \rho) : d(p, \mathcal{C}) \geq \rho + \epsilon\}$.

Thus, the machinable area of $\mathcal{P}$ w.r.t. ρ is exactly that subarea of $\mathcal{P}$ which can be machined by a tool with size ρ thereby keeping a margin with width ϵ. We remark that, for all $\rho > 0, \epsilon \geq 0$, $\mathcal{MA}(\mathcal{P}, \rho, \epsilon)$ necessarily is a true subset of $\mathcal{P}$ if $\mathcal{C}$ contains convex vertices.

Of course, we are interested in machining as much as possible. In the light of the previous remark we give the following definition.

Definition 8.8 (Totally Milled) For cutter sizes $\rho_1 < \rho_2$ and a margin width ϵ, the pocket $\mathcal{P}$ is *totally milled* by the tool path $\mathcal{TP}$ w.r.t. ρ_1, ρ_2, ϵ if $\mathcal{MA}(\mathcal{P}, \rho_1, \epsilon) = \mathcal{TS}(\mathcal{TP}_1, \rho_1) \cup \mathcal{TS}(\mathcal{TP}_2, \rho_2)$, where $\mathcal{TP} = \mathcal{TP}_1 \cup \mathcal{TP}_2$.

Algorithm Tool_Path($\downarrow$ *Area*, $\downarrow$ *Edge$_1$*, $\downarrow$ *Margin*, $\updownarrow$ $\mathcal{TP}$)
Begin
    machined_flag[*Area*] := **true**
    Edge$_2$:= *Edge$_1$*
    while *Offset*[*Area*] > *Margin* **do**
      Cutter_Pass($\downarrow$ *Edge$_2$*, $\downarrow$ *Offset*[*Area*], $\uparrow$ *C*, $\uparrow$ *Edge$_3$*)
      Adjoin *C* to $\mathcal{TP}$
      if *Edge$_1$* $\neq$ *Edge$_3$* **then**
        Let *New_Area* be that area which contains *Edge$_3$*
        Pop($\updownarrow$ *Offset_Stack*[*New_Area*], $\uparrow$ *Offset*[*New_Area*])
        Machine_Inwards($\downarrow$ *Edge$_3$*, $\downarrow$ *Offset*[*New_Area*], $\uparrow$ *C*)
        Adjoin *C* to $\mathcal{TP}$
        Tool_Path($\downarrow$ *New_Area*, $\downarrow$ *Edge$_3$*, $\downarrow$ *Offset*[*Area*], $\updownarrow$ $\mathcal{TP}$)
        Edge$_3$ $\uparrow$.*incident* := **false**
      else
        Pop($\updownarrow$ *Offset_Stack*[*Area*], $\uparrow$ *Offset*[*Area*])
        Machine_Outwards($\downarrow$ *Edge$_1$*, $\downarrow$ *Offset*[*Area*], $\uparrow$ *C*)
        Adjoin *C* to $\mathcal{TP}$
      end_if
      Edge$_2$:= *Edge$_3$*
    end_while
End Tool_Path.

Table 8.6: Algorithm Tool_Path.

Similarly, an area $\mathcal{A} \subseteq \mathcal{P}$ is called totally milled if the above equality holds when restricting both sides to $\mathcal{A}$.

Lemma 8.6 The pocket $\mathcal{P}$ is totally milled if every monotonous area of $\mathcal{P}$ is totally milled.

The following Correctness Lemma states that it is sufficient to ensure that every monotonous area of $\mathcal{P}$ has been entered in order guarantee that it has been totally machined.

Lemma 8.7 (Correctness Lemma) For a pocket $\mathcal{P}$, cutter sizes ρ_1, ρ_2 and margin width ϵ, the algorithm Tool_Path generates a tool path $\mathcal{TP}$ such that every monotonous area $\mathcal{A} \subseteq \mathcal{P}$ is totally milled w.r.t. ρ_1, ρ_2 and ϵ if $\mathcal{A}$ is entered by $\mathcal{TP}$.

Proof: Observe that, for every pass offset t associated with $\mathcal{A}$, the tool path $\mathcal{TP}$ generated by Tool_Path contains the cutter pass with offset t (restricted to $\mathcal{A}$), i.e. $OC(\mathcal{P}, \mathcal{C}, t) \cap \mathcal{A} \subseteq \mathcal{TP}$. Furthermore, all offsets are optimal. Thus, nothing is left uncut between two passes, which establishes the claim. $\square$

We summarize our results in the Main Correctness Theorem. It is an immediate consequence of the preceding lemmata and theorems of this chapter.

Theorem 8.2 (Main Correctness Theorem) For a pocket $\mathcal{P}$, cutter sizes ρ_1, ρ_2 and margin width ϵ, the algorithm Tool_Path generates a tool path $\mathcal{TP}$ such that $\mathcal{P}$ is totally milled w.r.t. ρ_1, ρ_2 and ϵ. Besides, all offsets are optimal.

Part III

Direction-parallel Milling

Chapter 9

Constructing the Mesh

Within this part, we will use the same terminology with respect to the pocket boundary as it has been introduced in the chapter on Voronoi diagrams. Additionally, the collection of negative islands is represented by the Jordan curves $\mathcal{N}_1, \ldots, \mathcal{N}_\nu$.

We suppose that offsets of the original border contour and of the positive islands are available. As stated in the survey chapter, the offset distance takes the form $\rho + \epsilon(\rho)$, where ρ as usual denotes the cutter radius and $\epsilon(\rho)$ stands for the width of the security margin at the boundary.

The following problems – which should be investigated with respect to the offsetted contours – are conceptually not different when referring to the original contours instead of the offsetted ones. Hence, for shorthand we do not explicitly refer to the offsetted contours. Rather, we carry out our investigation with respect to $\mathcal{P}$ and the original $\mathcal{B}$.

9.1   The Mesh

W.l.o.g. we assume that the requested inclination is zero, i.e. that the reference line of the zigzag segments is parallel to the x-axis. By convention, a line parallel to the x-axis with ordinate y is denoted by ℓ_y. Furthermore, for the sake of simplicity, we first restrict to pockets not containing negative islands. Handling negative islands will be explained in a subsequent section.

9.1.1   Definitions

Definition 9.1 (Zigzag Lines) For a pocket $\mathcal{P}$, let y_{min} and y_{max} denote the minimal and maximal y-coordinates of points of $\mathcal{B}$. Then, for a zigzag pass distance δ, the set $\mathcal{ZL}(\mathcal{P}, \delta)$ of *zigzag lines* w.r.t. $\mathcal{P}$ and δ (and $\mathcal{B}$) is the finite set of lines

$$\mathcal{ZL}(\mathcal{P}, \delta) := \{\ell_y : \ y = y_{min} + i \cdot \delta \ \wedge \ y \leq y_{max} \ \wedge \ i \in \mathbb{N}\}.$$

Definition 9.2 (Zigzag Segments) For a pocket $\mathcal{P}$ and a zigzag pass distance δ, the set $\mathcal{ZS}(\mathcal{P}, \delta)$ of *zigzag segments* is defined as

$$\mathcal{ZS}(\mathcal{P}, \delta) := \cup_{\ell \in \mathcal{ZL}(\mathcal{P},\delta)} \overline{\mathcal{P}} \cap \{\ell\}.$$

Hence, the zigzag segments are obtained by restricting the zigzag lines to the closure of $\mathcal{P}$. Clearly, we only deal with maximal zigzag segments, i.e. two zigzag segments that overlap are regarded as one single segment. The following definition establishes the nodes of our mesh.

Definition 9.3 (Nodes) The endpoints of zigzag segments are called *original nodes*. Local extrema of $\mathcal{B}$ (w.r.t. y-coordinates) are called *additional nodes*.

Definition 9.4 (Mesh) For a pocket $\mathcal{P}$ and a pass distance δ, the *mesh* $\mathcal{M}(\mathcal{P}, \delta)$ is an undirected graph whose set of nodes is the union of the original and the additional nodes. Two nodes of this graph are interconnected by an edge

1. if they are endpoints of the same zigzag segment, or
2. if they are located on the same contour and if it is possible to traverse this contour from one node to the second node thereby passing through no other node.

Edges of type 1 are called *horizontal* edges whereas edges of type 2 are called *vertical* edges.

Lemma 9.1 Every node of the graph $\mathcal{M}(\mathcal{P}, \delta)$ has at least two and at most three incident edges.

Proof: Since all nodes are members of Jordan curves, every node has exactly two incident vertical edges. By the same argument, an original node is a locus where a zigzag line exits $\mathcal{P}$. Hence, original nodes have exactly one incident horizontal edge, which establishes the claim. □

9.1.2 Implementational Issues

In order to achieve structural simplicity, we do not use variant records. Rather, every node is assigned four pointers to neighbouring nodes and a boolean value indicating whether it is an original or an additional node, cf. Table 9.1. Besides, the boolean flag *visited* will be used during the tool path generation. Additionally, some further data has to be stored (such as coordinates, incident contour objects, etc.).

9.2 Algorithm for Mesh Generation

9.2.1 Basic Outline

Computing the ordered sequence of intersections of a single line ℓ and an n-sided simple polygon can trivially be achieved by intersecting all edges of the polygon with ℓ and by arranging these intersections in sorted order along ℓ. This approach results in an $O(n \log n)$ algorithm, due to the complexity bound on sorting. By an elegant algorithm due to Hoffmann *et al*, it is possible to do this in only $O(n)$ time, cf. [H*85]. Their algorithm merely performs Jordan sorting by means of finger search trees.

type *Node_Ptr* = **pointer to** *Node_of_Mesh*

type *Node_of_Mesh* =
   record
      Up, Down: *Node_Ptr*
      Left, Right: *Node_Ptr*
      Coordinates: *Point*
      original_node: **Boolean**
      visited: **Boolean**
      additional data
   end_record

Table 9.1: Data Type *Node_of_Mesh*.

In order to obtain the zigzag segments, we have to repeatedly compute the intersections of parallel lines with $\mathcal{B}$. Hence, it seems to be appropriate to make use of the plane-sweep paradigm, cf. Preparata and Shamos' textbook [PS88]. In the sequel, we prepare for using a plane-sweep technique.

Given a pocket $\mathcal{P}$, consider drawing horizontal lines through the nodes of $\mathcal{M}(\mathcal{P}, \delta)$. This operation divides the plane into horizontal strips, commonly referred to as 'slabs'. Now consider the intersection of a slab with $\mathcal{B}$, which consists of portions of objects of $\mathcal{B}$. These portions constitute profiles[1] defining the sides of trapezoids. The following lemma confirms that a straight line parallel to the x-axis intersects every side of a trapezoid at most once.

Definition 9.5 A profile P is said to be *monotone* with respect to a straight line ℓ if every line orthogonal to ℓ intersects P at most in one point.

Lemma 9.2 Every maximal connected component of the intersection of $\mathcal{B}$ and the interior of a slab is monotone w.r.t. the y-axis.

Proof: Recall that $\mathcal{B}$ is subdivided at a number of points, including all local extrema w.r.t. y-coordinates.   □

Hence, the sweep-line paradigm can be applied, where the event-point schedule is given by the y-coordinates of the nodes of $\mathcal{M}(\mathcal{P}, \delta)$, and where the sweep-line status corresponds to the sequence of intersection intervals of the sweep-line and $\mathcal{B}$. By the previous lemma, when scanning the slabs in ascending order, this left-to-right sequence remains unaltered within a slab, but changes at the next slab boundary if an additional node is reached. Indeed, in this case the sweep-line status has to be updated by deleting or inserting sides of the trapezoids. At

---

[1] Remember Definition 5.20.

original nodes, the sweep-line status is precisely the sequence of **zigzag segments** of the corresponding zigzag line.

Since insertions and deletions have to be carried out, the sweep-line status is best represented as a height-balanced tree (e.g. an AVL-tree, cf. Wirth [Wir86], or a 2–3 tree, cf. Sedgewick [Sed88]), which, as it is well-known, supports insertions and deletions in time logarithmic in its size. The event-point schedule can simply be represented as an ordered list of points.

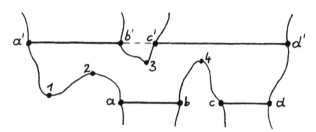

Figure 9.1: Generating the Mesh.

Consider the example depicted in Fig. 9.1 and suppose that the sweep-line is positioned at the zigzag line through points a and d, i.e. the sweep-line status represents the sequence of segments (a, b) and (c, d). Then, sweeping upwards we proceed as follows in order to establish the next segments (a', b') and (c', d'):

1. The local maxima 2 and 4 are deleted. Whereas deleting 2 has no effect, deleting 4 establishes the vertical edges between 4 and b, c and unifies the segments (a, b) and (c, d), yielding one new segment (a, d).

2. From the endpoints of all remaining segments, a search is directed upards for the original nodes at the next higher y-level. In our example, the search originates from a and d and reports a' and d'. Afterwards, the vertical edges between a and a' and d and d' are established. Besides, the segment (a', d') is located.

3. Then, the local minima 1 and 3 are inserted. Whereas inserting 1 has no effect, minimum 3 contributes the two original nodes b' and c', thereby transforming the sweep-line status into the two zigzag segments (a', b') and (c', d').

4. It remains to output the horizontal edges according to the sweep-line status.

A transformation of this description into a pseudo-code algorithm is straightforward and is left to the reader. Of course, the number of **zigzag segments** can differ from **zigzag** line to **zigzag** line.

9.2.2 Algorithm Complexity

From a complexity point of view, the work consists of insertions and deletions, each at a cost of $O(\log n)$, and of a generation of the output (i.e. drawing up the mesh). If there are κ zigzag lines, generating the output may take in total $O(n \cdot \kappa)$ time. Hence, we have proved the following complexity lemma.

Lemma 9.3 Generating the mesh for an n-sided pocket may take $O(n \cdot (\kappa + \log n))$ time, where κ denotes the number of zigzag lines.

9.2.3 Incorporating Negative Islands

Up to now, we have totally disregarded negative islands. Fortunately, it is not difficult to extend our scheme to this more general setting. Recall that negative islands are regions in the interior of the pocket which may be crossed by the tool. In other words, reserving space for a negative island is like placing an opaque layer on the zigzag path: the zigzag path under the layer (i.e. over the negative island) is still visible but it has perhaps changed its lightness.

As a matter of fact, intersections of zigzag lines with negative islands could simply be inserted after completion of the mesh. We prefer to use our above presented scheme for generating the mesh, which only has to be slightly modified: Instead of skipping those portions of a zigzag line which happen to lie above negative islands, these portions are also included into the mesh as horizontal edges. This means that original nodes lying on the boundary of a negative island have two incident horizontal edge. Besides, all nodes lying on the boundary of a negative island are flagged by a boolean value *negative_island*, which has to be added to our data type *Node_of_Mesh* presented in Table 9.1.

Incorporating negative islands in this way offers a further benefit: After the initial generation of the mesh, it is very easy to disactivate or reactivate negative islands interactively, without recomputing the mesh. Hence, generating the mesh can be regarded as a preprocessing step.

9.3 Computing a (Near) Optimum Inclination

9.3.1 Preparations

In the survey chapter, we have extensively motivated the importance of a suitable inclination. In the sequel, we state an algorithm for solving a closely related problem. Basically, we determine a reference line such that the number of lines which are tangent upon certain portions of $\mathcal{B}$ and which are parallel to this reference line is minimized.

Let ℓ^ψ denote a line inclined by the angle ψ w.r.t. the x-axis. We define $\chi(\mathcal{B}, \psi)$ as the number of points of reflex profiles of $\mathcal{B}$ that have tangents parallel to ℓ^ψ. Of course, in the case of a line segment $l \in \mathcal{B}$ parallel to ℓ^ψ, only one point out of $\bar{l}$ is counted. Hence, $\chi(\mathcal{B}, \psi)$ is linearly related to the number of local maxima and minima of $\mathcal{B}$ w.r.t. ℓ^ψ. For a definition of 'reflex profile', 'reflex arc', etc. recall Definition 5.23[2]. In particular, we remark that a reflex profile P is not terminated by vertices, i.e. P is an open curve. Then, we are solving the following problem:

Given: The boundary $\mathcal{B}$ of a pocket $\mathcal{P}$ (w.r.t. the canonical coordinate system).

Determine: An angle ϕ s.t. $\chi(\mathcal{B}, \phi) = \min_{0 \leq \psi \leq 2\pi} \chi(\mathcal{B}, \psi)$.

Clearly, it is not possible to obtain the result by a simple trial-and-error method because we would have to try an infinite number of angles. Rather, with every reflex profile we will associate an interval of 'recommended' angles. Scanning these intervals will finally yield a suitable ϕ. For the beginning, we examine some simple cases.

Lemma 9.4 Let $c \in \mathcal{B}$ be a reflex profile that consists of only one reflex circular arc. Furthermore, let v_s, v_e be the startpoint and the endpoint of c and denote the tangents upon c in v_s, v_e by ℓ_s, ℓ_e.

1. $\bar{c}$ is a semi-circle: In this case, $\ell_s = \ell_e$ is the only recommended reference line ℓ^ϕ s.t. no line parallel to ℓ^ϕ is tangent upon c in a point $p \in c$.

2. $\bar{c}$ is less than a semi-circle: In this case, every line through the intersection of ℓ_s and ℓ_e that also intersects c is a recommended reference line ℓ^ϕ.

3. $\bar{c}$ is more than a semi-circle, but less than a full circle: In this case, every line through the intersection of ℓ_s and ℓ_e which does not intersect the complement of $\bar{c}$ (w.r.t. the full circle containing c) is a recommended reference line ℓ^ϕ, i.e. no line parallel to ℓ^ϕ is tangent upon c in more than one point $p \in c$.

4. $\bar{c}$ is a full circle: every reference line ℓ^ϕ yields exactly two tangent points.

Proof: By a simple analysis according to the above cases. □

Lemma 9.5 Replacing a reflex profile P by a circular arc c does not alter $\chi(\mathcal{B}, \psi)$ if the tangent upon P in the endpoint of P is parallel to the tangent upon c in the endpoint of c, and if the tangent upon P in the startpoint of P is parallel to the tangent upon c in the startpoint of c.

---

[2]Our original definition is restricted to points, lines, and circular arcs. However, after subdividing general segments at their points of inflection, these definitions can readily be carried over to more general settings.

Proof: Observe that the inclinations of lines tangent upon P and c are identical. This establishes the claim.   □

9.3.2   Algorithm

Summarizing, we can associate an interval of recommended angles with every reflex profile $P \in \mathcal{B}$ by simply examining the inclinations of the tangent lines in the startpoint and the endpoint of P. Hence, if $\mathcal{B}$ has κ reflex profiles we get κ intervals $[a_1..b_1], \ldots, [a_\kappa..b_\kappa]$. W.l.o.g. we may assume that $[a_i..b_i] \subset [0..\pi[$ for $1 \leq i \leq \kappa$. What remains to do is to select an angle ϕ such that $\chi(\mathcal{B}, \phi)$ is minimal.

This task is executed by the following algorithm Determine_Inclination, cf. Table 9.2, which is similar to the procedure Measure_of_Union_of_Intervals stated by Preparata and Shamos, cf. [PS88]. The input to this algorithm consists of the angles $a_1, b_1, \ldots, a_n, b_n$ sorted into the array $Angles[1..2\kappa]$. Additionally, $Angles$ must obey the property that, if a_m is placed in $Angles[\mu]$, b_n is placed in $Angles[\nu]$, and $a_m = b_n$ then $\mu < \nu$. Thus, in order to guarantee an overlap, a lower bound of an interval has to be placed before an upper bound of the same numerical value.

Algorithm Determine_Inclination($\downarrow$ *Angles*, $\uparrow [a..b]$)
Begin
    $j := 0$
    for $i := 1$ **to** 2κ **do**
      if *Angles*[i] is a lower bound **then**
        $j := j + 1$
      else
        $j := j - 1$
      End
      Multiplicity[i] := j
    end_for
    Let i s.t. *Multiplicity*[i] is maximal
    $a := Angles[i]$
    $b := Angles[i+1]$
End Determine_Inclination.

Table 9.2: Algorithm Determine_Inclination.

Algorithm Determine_Inclination determines the multiplicities of overlapping intervals and stores them in the array $Multiplicity[1..2\kappa]$. After assigning the multiplicities to all bounds, a simple scan through this array reveals the (sub)interval $[a..b]$ of angles such that $\chi(\mathcal{B}, \phi)$ is minimal for $\phi \in [a..b]$. Of course, $[a..b]$ may degenerate to a singleton.

The major drawback of this approach – besides the fact that it does not guarantee to find the best inclination – is its numerical instability. The request to place lower bounds before upper bounds is difficult to realize in practice because it involves a test for equality of real values. In our own implementation ZIGPOCKET, we faced some odd problems when rotating the sample example depicted in Fig. 3.2 for a number of times, thereby using random rotation angles. However, rather 'dirty' tricks helped to overcome most effects caused by this numerical problem.

Chapter 10

Generating the Tool Path

10.1   Algorithm for Tool Path Generation

10.1.1   Basic Outline

In the survey chapter on zigzag machining we have already stated the main ideas for generating the tool path. The main principle is to work entirely on the mesh. The actual heart of this process is constituted by the following three tasks:

1. Move along a zigzag line segment, i.e. move along an horizontal edge between two original nodes.

2. Determine the next two original nodes at a lower/higher y-level for which task 1 has to be executed.

3. Move along portions of $\mathcal{B}$ in order to get from the old y-level to the next y-level.

Whereas tasks 1 and 3 are more or less trivial, task 2 needs a careful treatment in order to ensure that the pocket $\mathcal{P}$ is totally milled.

Suppose that the tool has been moved from the original node *Left_Node* to the original node *Right_Node* and is to move upwards, i.e. the next pair of nodes (*Left_Node, Right_Node*) is to be determined. The overall structure of an algorithm solving this problem is stated in Table 10.1. The algorithm Upwards_Right examines whether the upwards pointer of *Right_Node* points to an original node. If this is true, the next right node has been found. Otherwise, the algorithm Mill_Upwards_Right is envoked which scans over additional nodes until the upwards pointer of the actual *Right_Node* points to an original node. During this scan all entries to possibly not yet machined areas are pushed onto a stack.

The algorithm Search_Upwards_Left is similar to Mill_Upwards_Right, with 'left' and 'right' properly exchanged, except that the intermediate nodes must not be flagged as *visited*. Besides, minor differences occur in the way nodes are pushed on the stack.

Summarizing, relying on the mesh a tool path can be generated undertaking few efforts. In the case of a dead end, the tool has to be lifted and moved to the next area to be machined, which is identified by popping its entry nodes from the stack. Flagging already visited nodes prevents machining areas twice. For machining the whole pocket according to this scheme, the corresponding algorithm *Zigzag_Path* is stated in Table 10.3.

Zigzag_Path is initially called with *Left_Node, Right_Node* pointing to those original nodes which are immediately above the global minimum of $\mathcal{C}_0$. The single upwards scans are executed by algorithm Upwards, cf. Table 10.4, which in turn makes use of Upwards_Right and Upwards_Left. The algorithm Downwards is totally symmetric to Upwards and is therefore omitted.

Algorithm Upwards_Right($\updownarrow$ *Left_Node*, $\updownarrow$ *Right_Node*, $\uparrow$ *dead_end*)
Begin
    dead_end := **false**
    Left_Node$\uparrow$.*visited* := **true**
    Right_Node$\uparrow$.*visited* := **true**
    Right_Node := *Right_Node*$\uparrow$.*Up*
    Output_Path($\downarrow$ *Right_Node*)
    if $\neg$ *Right_Node*$\uparrow$.*original_node* **then**
      if *Right_Node* is a dead end **then**
        dead_end := **true**
      else
        Mill_Upwards_Right($\updownarrow$ *Right_Node*, $\updownarrow$ *dead_end*)
      end_if
    end_if
    Left_Node := *Left_Node*$\uparrow$.*Up*
    if $\neg$ *Left_Node*$\uparrow$.*original_node* **then**
      Search_Upwards_Left($\updownarrow$ *Left_Node*)
    end_if
End Upwards_Right.

Table 10.1: Algorithm Upwards_Right.

In the stated versions, algorithm Zigzag_Path and its subalgorithms lack particular care about technological requirements. For instance, after retracting the tool the new starting point should not randomly be selected between *Left_Node* and *Right_Node*. Rather, in order to achieve a minimal number of predrill positions, only that node should be selected which has already been visited by the tool path. Besides, the tool should plunge down onto the material thereby keeping some safety distance towards the unmachined regions; i.e. when plunging down the tool, the tool center point and the node should not be identical.

As demonstrated by our practical implementation ZIGPOCKET, it is rather easy to modify the schemes presented above in order to cope with these requirements arising from practice. However, for the sake of a simplified description we have omitted these details.

Algorithm Mill_Upwards_Right($\updownarrow$ *Right_Node*, $\updownarrow$ *dead_end*)
Begin
    Left_Node := *Right_Node*$\uparrow$.*Down*
    Right_Node := *Left_Node*$\uparrow$.*Right*
    Left_Node$\uparrow$.*visited* := **true**
    Right_Node$\uparrow$.*visited* := **true**
    Push *Left_Node*$\uparrow$.*Down*, *Right_Node*$\uparrow$.*Down*, *downwards* onto stack
    Right_Node := *Right_Node*$\uparrow$.*Up*
    Output_Path($\downarrow$ *Right_Node*)
    if ¬ *Right_Node*$\uparrow$.*original_node* **then**
      if *Right_Node* is a dead end **then**
        dead_end := **true**
      else
        Mill_Upwards_Right($\updownarrow$ *Right_Node*, $\updownarrow$ *dead_end*)
      end_if
    end_if
End Mill_Upwards_Right.

Table 10.2: Algorithm Mill_Upwards_Right.

Algorithm Zigzag_Path($\downarrow$ *Left_Node*, $\downarrow$ *Right_Node*)
Begin
    Upwards($\downarrow$ *Left_Node*, $\downarrow$ *Right_Node*)
    while stack is not empty **do**
      Pop *Left_Node*, *Right_Node*, and *direction* from the stack
      if ¬ *Left_Node*$\uparrow$.*visited* **then**
        if *direction* = *upwards* **then**
          Upwards($\downarrow$ *Left_Node*, $\downarrow$ *Right_Node*)
        else
          Downwards($\downarrow$ *Left_Node*, $\downarrow$ *Right_Node*)
        end_if
      end_if
    end_while
End Zigzag_Path.

Table 10.3: Algorithm Zigzag_Path.

Algorithm Upwards($\downarrow$ *Left_Node*, $\downarrow$ *Right_Node*)
Begin
    switch := 0
    repeat
      if Odd($\downarrow$ *switch*) **then**
        Upwards_Right($\updownarrow$ *Left_Node*, $\updownarrow$ *Right_Node*, $\uparrow$ *dead_end*)
      else
        Upwards_Left($\updownarrow$ *Left_Node*, $\updownarrow$ *Right_Node*, $\uparrow$ *dead_end*)
      End
      switch := *switch* + 1
    until *dead_end*
End Upwards.

Table 10.4: Algorithm Upwards.

10.1.2 Correctness

Lemma 10.1 (Termination) For a pocket $\mathcal{P}$, the algorithm Zigzag_Path terminates.

Proof: For each call of Upwards or Downwards, at least two original nodes are flagged *finished*. Since Zigzag_Path envokes Upwards and Downwards only for unflagged nodes and there is only a finite number of nodes, Zigzag_Path terminates provided that Upwards and Downwards terminate. The proof of their termination is straightforward. $\qquad\Box$

In order to correctly reflect the zigzag problem, we redefine the term 'totally milled'.

Definition 10.1 The pocket $\mathcal{P}$ is called *totally milled* w.r.t. the mesh $\mathcal{M}(\mathcal{P}, \delta)$ if every horizontal edge of $\mathcal{M}(\mathcal{P}, \delta)$ has been traversed by the tool.

Lemma 10.2 After the execution of the algorithm Zigzag_Path, a horizontal edge of the mesh $\mathcal{M}(\mathcal{P}, \delta)$ has been traversed by the tool if one of its endnodes has been flagged *visited*.

Proof: An inspection of Zigzag_Path and its subalgorithms reveals that only the input nodes of the algorithm Upwards_Right and its siblings are flagged *visited*. However, the algorithm Upwards_Right causes the tool to move from the input *Left_Node* to the input *Right_Node*, establishing the claim. $\qquad\Box$

Lemma 10.3 The mesh $\mathcal{M}(\mathcal{P}, \delta)$ is a connected graph.

Proof: Let $v_1 \neq v_2$ be nodes of $\mathcal{M}(\mathcal{P}, \delta)$. W.l.o.g. assume that both nodes are original ones.

Case: $v_1 \in \mathcal{C}$ and $v_2 \in \mathcal{C}$, for a curve $\mathcal{C} \in \mathcal{B}$. Obviously, it is possible to travel around $\mathcal{C}$ by means of the upwards and downwards pointers, i.e. there exists a path on the mesh between v_1 and v_2.

Case: $v_1 \in \mathcal{C}_i$, $v_2 \in \mathcal{C}_j$ and $\mathcal{C}_i \neq \mathcal{C}_j \in \mathcal{B}$. Then we proceed as follows: If $i = 0$, i.e. v_1 lies on the border contour, then we are finished. Otherwise, we construct a path between v_1 and a node on $\mathcal{C}_0$. Move along $\mathcal{C}_i$, until a node $v_1' \in \mathcal{C}_i$ is detected s.t. v_1' is a left endnode of a horizontal edge e. Such a node must exist because $\mathcal{C}_i$ lies in the interior of $\mathcal{C}_0$ and $\mathcal{C}_i$ is a Jordan curve. Let v_1'' be the right endnode of e. If $v_1'' \in \mathcal{C}_0$, then we are finished. Otherwise, the same search process is applied to v_1'' instead of v_1. Hence, we end up with paths between v_1, v_2 and nodes on $\mathcal{C}_0$. According to the previous case, a path between v_1 and v_2 can therefore be constructed.   □

Lemma 10.4 In the course of execution of the algorithm Zigzag_Path, every original node is flagged *visited*.

Proof: Let v be a node of the mesh and suppose that it is not flagged after the termination of Zigzag_Path.

Case: $v \in \mathcal{C}_0$. Observe that the original node encountered next when traversing $\mathcal{C}_0$ in CCW order cannot be flagged because otherwise v would have been either visited or pushed on the stack. Hence, no original node of $\mathcal{C}_0$ can be flagged, which contradicts the fact that Zigzag_Path is initially called with nodes being elements of $\mathcal{C}$. Similarly, if one original node of an island contour has not been flagged, then all original nodes of this contour cannot be flagged.

Case: $v \in \mathcal{C}_i$ and $i > 0$. Consider the right-hand portion r of the zigzag line through v and denote the rightmost intersection of r and $\mathcal{C}_0$ by v'. Since v' is flagged, the left endnode v'' of the horizontal edge through v' is flagged. Therefore, the whole contour v'' lies on is flagged. In particular, the rightmost intersection v''' of r with $\mathcal{B}$ except v', v'' is flagged. By applying the same argument to v''' instead of v', we learn that v must be flagged.   □

We summarize our results in the following Correctness Theorem.

Theorem 10.1 (Correctness Theorem) For a pocket $\mathcal{P}$ and a mesh $\mathcal{M}(\mathcal{P}, \delta)$, the algorithm Zigzag_Path terminates and generates a tool path s.t. $\mathcal{P}$ is totally milled w.r.t. $\mathcal{M}(\mathcal{P}, \delta)$.

10.2 Handling Negative Islands

Handling negative islands requires a great deal of caution because inproper commands for rapid feed moves can result in a tool breakage. Since we do not impose restrictions on the shape of negative islands – except that they have to be bounded by Jordan curves and must not intersect pairwaise – a rather complex scheme is necessary for properly handling negative islands. In particular, a lot of special cases have to be considered.

Unfortunately, strategies for handling negative islands are subject to a lot of technological considerations, which may vary from application to application. Hence, there exists no strategy which is uniquely best. This is the main reason why we content ourselves to a rough sketch of our approach. Our approach is meant to be flexible enough in order that it can be adapted to diverse technological requirements.

Algorithm Negative_Island_Left, cf. Table 10.5 presents the overall structure of our approach. Suppose that we are to determine the rapid feed moves of a tool with radius ρ moving along the zigzag line ℓ from right to left. Furthermore, suppose that ℓ partially lies above the negative island $\mathcal{N}$. W.l.o.g. we assume that ℓ intersects $\mathcal{N}$ in only two points p_L, p_R, i.e. $\ell \cap \mathcal{N} = \{p_L, p_R\}$. Let $\mathcal{N}^* := \mathcal{N} \setminus (\mathcal{N} \cap \mathcal{TS}(\mathcal{TP}, \rho))$, where $\mathcal{TP}$ denotes the already generated tool path. Thus, $\mathcal{N}^*$ is that portion of $\mathcal{N}$ which has not yet been covered by the cutter circle when moving along the tool path.

Algorithm Negative_Island_Left($\downarrow \epsilon_1, \downarrow \epsilon_2, \downarrow \rho, \downarrow p_L, \downarrow p_R, \downarrow \ell, \downarrow \mathcal{N}^*$)
Begin
    $p := p_R$
    while $p \neq p_L$ **do**
       Move_Until $p = p_L \;\vee\; C(p, \rho + \epsilon_1) \cap \mathcal{N}^* = \emptyset$
       Rapid_Move_Until $p = p_L \;\vee\; C(p, \rho + \epsilon_2) \cap \mathcal{N}^* \neq \emptyset$
    end_while
End Negative_Island_Left.

Table 10.5: Algorithm Negative_Island_Left.

The commands Move_Until and Rapid_Move_Until are similar to the statements for sensor-controlled move, which are supported by modern robot programming languages, cf. Blume and Jakob [BJ83,BJ86,BJF87]. The point p is associated with the actual position during the move. The variables ϵ_1, ϵ_2 represent safety distances which have to be kept at the entrance to and the exit of a negative island. Sometimes, it is only required that the front half of the tool does not intersect with the island contour in order to allow a rapid feed movement. In this case, the condition in the Move_Until statements has to be modified.

How can we simulate the sensor-controlled moves by means of algorithms entirely relying on the available geometric data? The key to success is provided by offsetting $\mathcal{N}$ by the offsets $\rho + \epsilon_1, \rho + \epsilon_2$. Intersecting $OC(\mathcal{N}, \rho + \epsilon_i)$ with ℓ yields a number of event points which may correspond to changes between non-cutting rapid feed moves and cutting moves. Sorting these points in a right-to-left order yields a number of possibly overlapping intervals of ℓ, each of which corresponds either to a rapid feed move or to a normal move.

Based on this structure, it is straightforward to design an algorithm that determines the intervals for rapid feed moves. Basically, the union of all intervals corresponding to normal moves is computed; the complement (w.r.t. ℓ and $\mathcal{N}$) yields the rapid feed moves. However, care has to be taken that only that portion of $OC(\mathcal{N}, \rho + \epsilon_2)$ is considered for intersection with ℓ which corresponds to the offset of $\mathcal{N}^*$.

Appendix A

Examples

In this appendix, we present some sample pocketing tasks handled by our program package GEOPOCKET/ZIGPOCKET. All calculations have been performed on a DEC VAX 8350[1] running VMS. The pocketing examples are numbered and the corresponding CPU-times are assembled in two tables, according to the pocketing strategy used. All CPU-times have been measured in milliseconds.

Throughout the following plots[2], pocket contours are depicted by thick solid lines; thin solid lines stand for the cutter paths; thin dashed lines indicate rapid feed moves; and moves in the air are depicted by dotted-dashed lines. The depicted full circles correspond to the tools used for milling.

A.1 Contour-parallel Milling

The following Table A.1 summarizes the CPU-consumptions for processing the sample pockets No. 1–9. The CPU-consumption of the computation of the Voronoi diagram of a multiply-connected pocket is listed in column $\mathcal{VD}_1$, whereas column $\mathcal{VD}_2$ corresponds to the computation of the Voronoi diagram of a (pseudo) simply-connected pocket[3]. The column 'Area' corresponds to the computations of the monotonous areas. The efforts for determining optimal offsets are listed in the column 'Offset', and the column $\mathcal{TP}$ corresponds to the final computations of the tool paths. For each pocket, the number $\#(\mathcal{B})$ of boundary objects (contributing to $\mathcal{VD}(\mathcal{B})$) and the number $\#(\mathcal{TP})$ of tool path elements are listed.

---

[1]Under moderate working load, the performance of this multi-user system offered to the individual user can roughly be compared to the performance of a (slow) VAXstation 2000.

[2]The assistance of Andreas Maier in generating these plots is gratefully acknowledged.

[3]Recall the transformation of the contours outlined in the survey chapter on contour-parallel milling. As a matter of principle, recomputing the Voronoi diagram of a pseudo simply-connected pocket area could be avoided by performing local updates of the diagram of the original multiply-connected pocket. However, due to lack of time this update has not been implemented. In the figures, the Voronoi diagrams corresponding to the original pockets are plotted.

CPU-Time Statistics								
No.	$\#(\mathcal{B})$	$\#(\mathcal{TP})$	$\mathcal{VD}_1$	$\mathcal{VD}_2$	Area	Offset	$\mathcal{TP}$	Total
1	32	128	—	1000	330	490	360	2180
2	122	337	—	2290	440	1800	510	5040
3	160	592	—	3620	370	2520	710	7220
4	174	616	4310	3960	520	2710	720	12220
5	57	283	1470	1150	410	1170	680	4880
6	100	290	2040	1620	370	900	610	5540
7	110	349	3200	3130	480	1450	650	8910
8	55	346	1220	900	420	1580	540	4460
9	98	615	4690	3280	490	2730	740	11930

Table A.1: CPU-Time Statistics for Contour-parallel Milling.

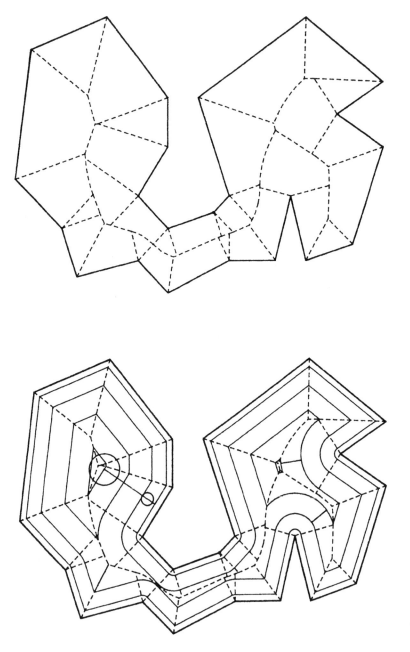

Figure A.1: Pocketing Example No. 1

Figure A.2: Pocketing Example No. 2

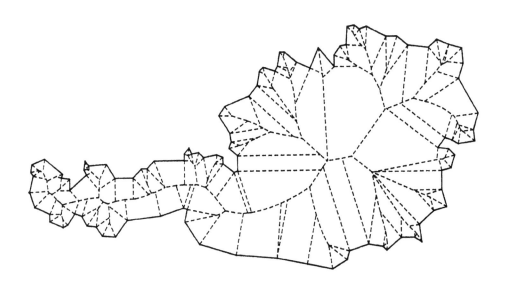

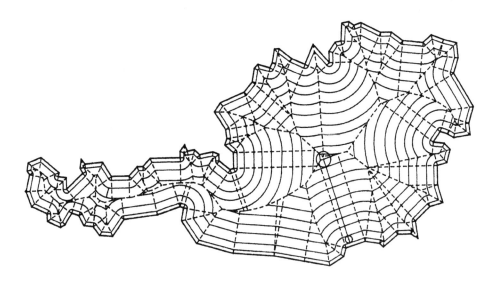

Figure A.3: Pocketing Example No. 3

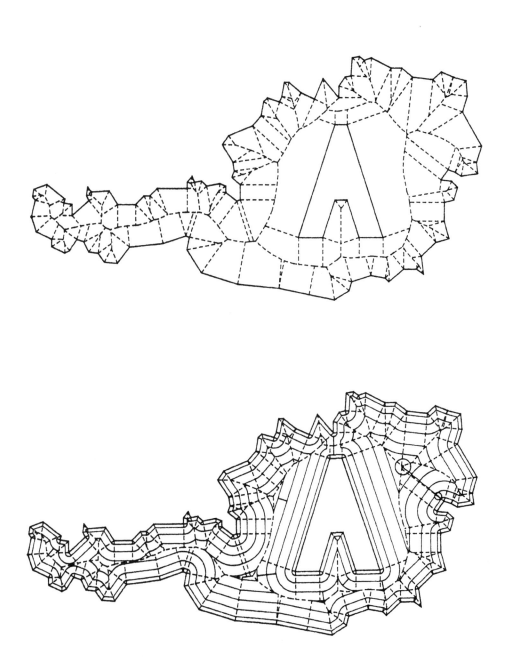

Figure A.4: Pocketing Example No. 4

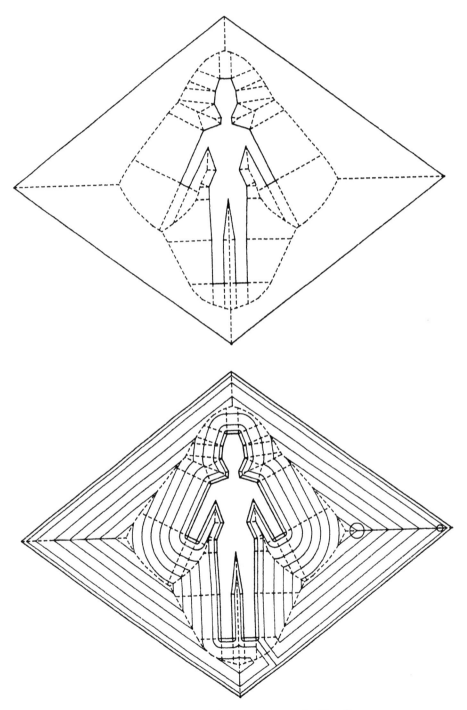

Figure A.5: Pocketing Example No. 5

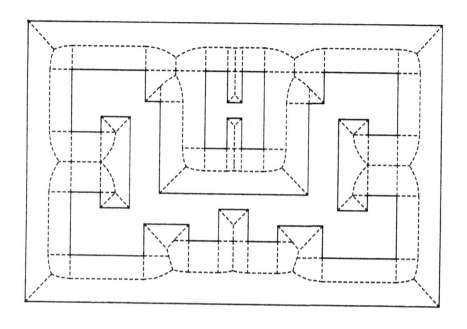

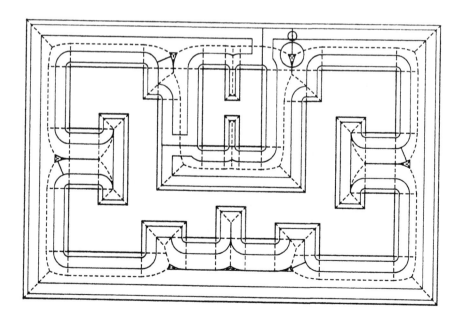

Figure A.6: Pocketing Example No. 6

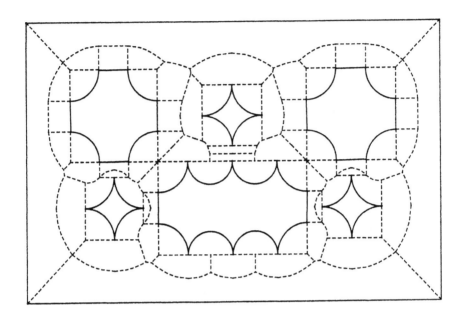

Figure A.7: Pocketing Example No. 7

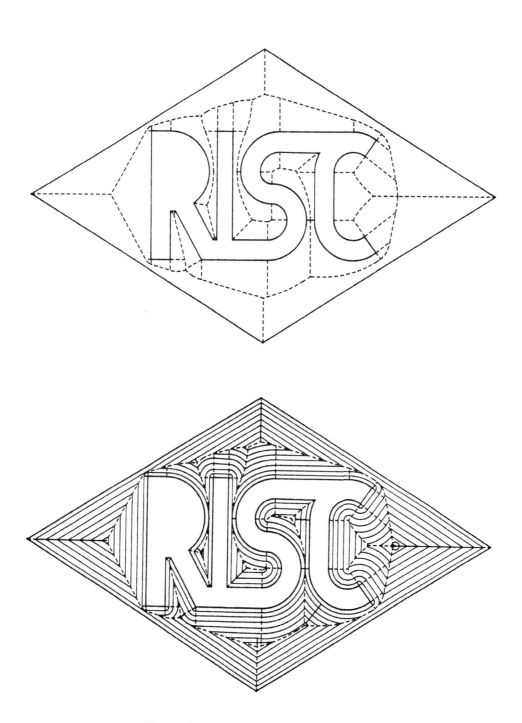

Figure A.8: Pocketing Example No. 8

Figure A.9: Pocketing Example No. 9

A.2 Direction-parallel Milling

The following Table A.2 summarizes the CPU-consumptions for processing the sample pockets No. 10–17. The CPU-consumptions of the computations of the outmost offset curves[4] are listed in column 'Curve'. The column 'Inclin' corresponds to the determinations of suitable inclinations. The efforts for generating the meshes are listed in the column 'Mesh', and column $\mathcal{TP}$ corresponds to the final computation of the tool paths.

CPU-Time Statistics							
No.	#($\mathcal{B}$)	#($\mathcal{TP}$)	Curve	Inclin	Mesh	$\mathcal{TP}$	Total
10	160	148	3710	80	360	370	4520
11	41	168	1460	30	380	390	2260
12	100	279	2140	60	510	590	3300
13	55	223	360	30	520	580	1490
14	110	263	3320	60	590	420	4390
15	55	267	1310	10	520	440	2280
16	100	197	370	10	610	630	1620
17	98	239	4720	90	540	440	5790

Table A.2: CPU-Time Statistics for Direction-parallel Milling.

---

[4]These curves have been generated by means of Voronoi diagrams. In order to highlight the zigzag patterns, the Voronoi diagrams have not been plotted in the figures.

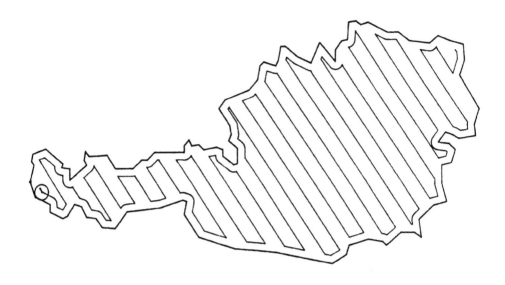

Figure A.10: Pocketing Example No. 10

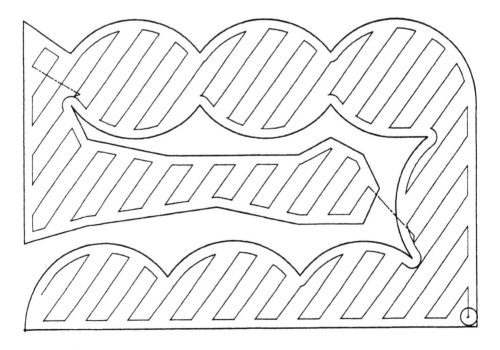

Figure A.11: Pocketing Example No. 11

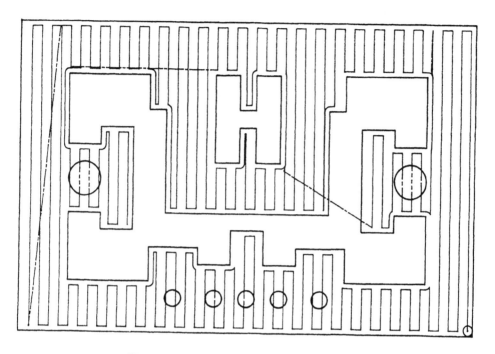

Figure A.12: Pocketing Example No. 12

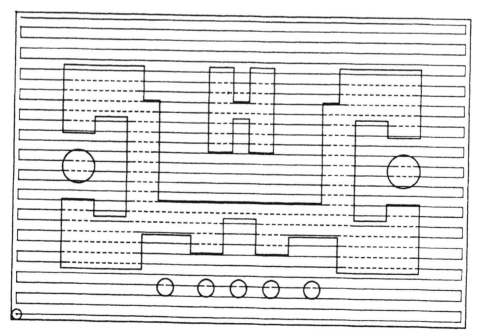

Figure A.13: Pocketing Example No. 13

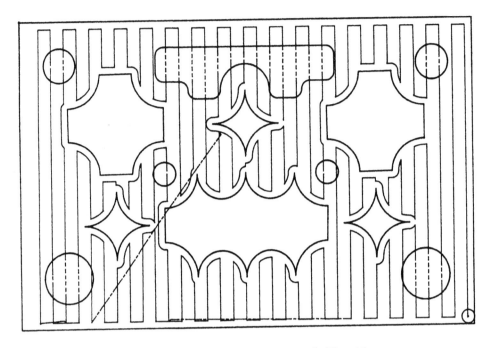

Figure A.14: Pocketing Example No. 14

Figure A.15: Pocketing Example No. 15

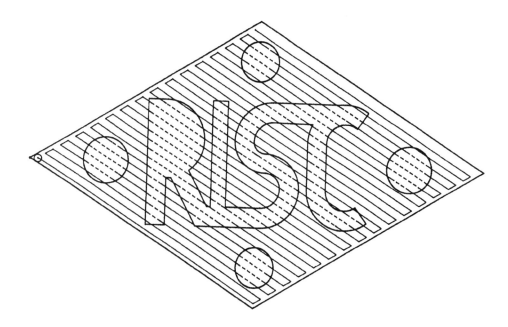

Figure A.16: Pocketing Example No. 16

Figure A.17: Pocketing Example No. 17

List of Figures

List of Tables

Bibliography

[A*74]   A.V. Aho et al. *The Design and Analysis of Computer Algorithms*. Addison-Wesley, Reading, MA, USA, 1974.

[AB83]   D. Avis and B.K. Bhattacharya.   Algorithms for Computing *d*-dimensional Voronoi Diagrams and their Duals. In F.P. Preparata (ed.), *Advances in Computing Research: Computational Geometry*, p. 159–180, JAI Press, Greenwich, CT, USA, 1983.

[Aur88] F. Aurenhammer. *Voronoi Diagrams – A Survey*.   Technical Report 263, TU Graz, Austria, November 1988.

[Baa88] S. Baase. *Computer Algorithms*. Addison-Wesley, Reading, MA, USA, second ed., 1988. (ISBN 0-201-06035-3).

[Bau74] B.G. Baumgart. *Geometric Modeling for Computer Vision*. Technical Report STAN-CS-74-463, Artificial Intelligence Lab, Stanford U., Stanford, CA, USA, 1974.

[Bau75] B.G. Baumgart.   A Polyhedral Representation for Computer Vision. In *Proc. National Computer Science Conference*, p. 44:589–596, AFIPS Press, Arlington, VA, USA, 1975.

[Bez70] P. Bézier. *Emploi des machines à commande numérique*. Masson et Cie, Paris, France, 1970. (Translated by A.R. Forrest and A.F. Pankhurst as *Numerical Control – Mathematics and Applications*, John Wiley & Sons, New York, USA).

[BJ83]   C. Blume and W. Jakob. Design of the Structured Robot Language (SRL). In *Proc. Advanced Software for Robotics*, Liège, France, 1983.

[BJ86]   C. Blume and W. Jakob. *Programming Languages for Industrial Robots*. *Symbolic Computation – Artificial Intelligence*, Springer-Verlag, 1986.

[BJF87]   C. Blume, W. Jakob, and J. Favaro. *PasRo: Pascal and C for Robots.* Springer-Verlag, second ed., 1987.

[Blu67]   H. Blum. A Model for Extracting New Descriptors of Shape. In W.W. Dunn (ed.), *Models for the Perception of Speech and Visual Form*, p. 289–310, MIT Press, Cambridge, MA, USA, 1967.

[Blu74]   H. Blum. A Geometry for Biology. *Math. Analysis of Fundamental Biological Phenomena*, 231(1):19–30, 1974.

[Bru82]   L.K. Bruckner. Geometric Algorithms for $2\frac{1}{2}$D Roughing Process of Sculptured Surfaces. In *Proc. Joint Anglo-Hungarian Seminar on Computer-Aided Geometric Design*, Budapest, Hungary, October 1982.

[BZ84]   B.E. Barkoczy and W.J. Zdeblick. A Knowledge-Based System for Machining Operation Planning. In *Proc. CASA/SME AUTOFACT 6 Conf.*, p. 2.11–2.23, Anaheim, CA, USA, 1984.

[C*84]   B.K. Choi et al. Automatic Recognition of Machined Surfaces from $3D$ Solid Model. *Computer-Aided Design*, 16(2):81–86, March 1984.

[Can87]   J.F. Canny. *The Complexity of Robot Motion. ACM – MIT Press Doctoral Dissertation Award Series*, MIT Press, Cambridge, MA, USA, 1987. (ISBN 0-262-03136-1).

[CB85]   B.K. Choi and M.M. Barash. STOPP: An Approach to CAD/CAM Integration. *Computer-Aided Design*, 17(4):162–168, May 1985.

[CD88]   J.F. Canny and B. Donald. Simplified Voronoi Diagrams. *Discrete and Computational Geometry*, 3(3):219–236, 1988.

[Cze76a] N. Czeranowsky. *Anleitung zur Berechnung des "bezogenen Zeilenabstandes" beim Zeilenfräsen ebener Flächen (A Guide to the Calculation of a Related Cutter Pass Distance for the Offset Curve Milling of Planar Areas).* Technical Report, IFW, TU Hannover, FRG, September 1976.

[Cze76b] N. Czeranowsky. NC-Taschenfräsen aus dem vollen Werkstoff – Anwendung der APT-Pocket-Routine (NC-Pocket Machining – Applying the APT-POCKET-Routine). *Werkstatt und Betrieb*, 109(8):459–463, 1976.

[Die84]   H. Diedenhoven. *Anwendung von Algorithmen der rechnerunterstützten Konstruktion zur Ermittlung kollisionsfreier Werkzeugwege für*

NC-Maschinen mit fünf Bewegungsachsen (Application of CAD Techniques for the Generation of Collision-free Tool Paths for NC Machines with Five Axes). Technical Report, Inst. für Konstruktionstechnik, Ruhr-Universität Bochum, Bochum, FRG, September 1984.

[Dir50]   G.L. Dirichlet. Über die Reduktion der positiven quadratischen Formen mit drei unbestimmten ganzen Zahlen. *J. Reine u. Angew. Math.*, 40:209–227, 1850.

[DL81]   Y. Descotte and J.L. Latombe. GARI: A Problem Solver that Plans How to Machine Mechanical Parts. In *Proc. 8th IJCAI*, Vancouver, Canada, 1981.

[DL84]   Y. Descotte and J.L. Latombe. An Expert System for Process Planning. In M.S. Picket and J.W. Boyse (eds.), *Solid Modeling by Computers: From Theory to Applications*, p. 329–346, Plenum Press, New York, USA, 1984.

[Dry79]   R.L. Drysdale. *Generalized Voronoi Diagrams and Geometric Searching*. Technical Report STAN-CS-79-705, Dept. of Computer Science, Stanford U., Stanford, CA, USA, 1979. (PhD thesis).

[Ede87]   H. Edelsbrunner. *Algorithms in Combinatorial Geometry. EATCS Monographs on Theoretical Computer Science*, Springer-Verlag, 1987.

[FN89]   R.T. Farouki and C.A. Neff. *Some Analytic and Algebraic Properties of Plane Offset Curves*. Technical Report RC-14364, IBM Thomas J. Watson Research Center, Yorktown Heights, NY, USA, January 1989.

[For71]   A.R. Forrest. Computational Geometry. *Proc. Royal Society London*, 312(4):187–195, 1971.

[For85]   S. Fortune. *A Sweepline Algorithm for Voronoi Diagrams*. Technical Report, AT&T Bell Laboratories, Murray Hill, NJ, USA, December 1985.

[For86]   S. Fortune. A Sweepline Algorithm for Voronoi Diagrams. In *Proc. 2nd Annual ACM Symposium on Computational Geometry*, p. 313–323, 1986.

[For87a]   A.R. Forrest. Computational Geometry and Software Engineering: Towards a Geometric Computing Environment. In D.F. Rogers and R.A. Earnshaw (eds.), *Techniques for Computer Graphics*, p. 23–37, Springer-Verlag, 1987. (ISBN 3-540-96492-4).

[For87b]   S. Fortune. A Sweepline Algorithm for Voronoi Diagrams. *Algorith-mica*, 2(2):153–174, 1987.

[G*85]   M. Grötschel et al. *Geometric Algorithms and Combinatorial Opti-mization*. Springer-Verlag, second ed., 1985. (ISBN 3-540-13624-X).

[G*88]   D.C. Genord et al. An Automatic NC Processor: Harnessing the Technology of Form Feature Based Solids Modeling. In *Proc. AUTO-FACT'88*, p. 11.1–11.11, Society of Manufacturing Engineers, Com-puter and Automated Systems Association (CASA/SME), Chicago, IL, USA, November 1988.

[GH81]   G. Geise and S. Harms. Approximation ebener Kurven durch Kreis-bogenzüge (Approximation of Planar Curves by Piecewise Circular Curves). *Hefte des WBZ MKR/IV TU Dresden*, 48/81:41–46, 1981.

[Gra75]   A.R. Grayer. *The Automatic Production of Machined Components Starting from a Stored Geometric Description*. Technical Report 88, CAD Group, Cambridge U., Cambridge, UK, July 1975.

[Gur89]   H.N. Gürsoy. *Shape Interrogation by Medial Axis Transform for Auto-mated Analysis*. PhD thesis, MIT, Dept. of Ocean Engineering, Cam-bridge, MA, USA, November 1989.

[Guy89]   M.K. Guyder. Automating the Optimization of $2\frac{1}{2}$ Axis Milling. In F. Kimura and A. Rolstadås (eds.), *Proc. Computer Applications in Production and Engineering (CAPE'89)*, North-Holland, Amsterdam, NL, October 1989.

[GZ84]   M.P. Groover and E.W. Zimmers. *CAD/CAM: Computer-Aided De-sign and Manufacturing*. Prentice-Hall, Englewood Cliffs, NJ, USA, 1984. (ISBN 0-13-110130-7).

[H*85]   K. Hoffmann et al. Sorting Jordan Sequences in Linear Order. In *Proc. ACM Symposium on Computational Geometry*, p. 196–203, June 1985.

[HA88]   A. Hansen and F. Arbab. *An Algorithm for Generating NC Tool Paths for Arbitrarily Shaped Pockets with Islands*. Technical Report CS 88-51, CS Dept., U. of Southern California, Los Angeles, CA, USA, 1988.

[Har80]   D. Harenbrock. *Die Kopplung von rechnerunterstützter Konstruk-tion und Fertigung mit dem Programmbaustein PROREN 1/NC (The Connection of CAD and CAM by Means of the Program Package PROREN1/NC)*. Technical Report, Inst. für Konstruktionstechnik, Ruhr-Universität Bochum, Bochum, FRG, 1980.

[Heg88]   G. Hégron. *Image Synthesis.* MIT Press, Cambridge, MA, USA, 1988. (ISBN 0-262-08166-0).

[Hel87a]   M. Held. Extensions and Improvements of a Pocket Machining Algorithm by Means of Computational Geometry. In G. Pernul and A. Min Tjoa (eds.), *Proc. Berichte aus Informatikforschungsinstitutionen,* p. 477–486, Schriftenreihe OCG, Vol. 37, Oldenbourg Verlag, February 1987.

[Hel87b]   M. Held. *Fully Automated Pocket Machining by Means of Computational Geometry.* Master's thesis, Technical Report No. 87-23.0 (RISC-Linz Series), Inst. für Mathematik, J. Kepler U. Linz, Linz, Austria, September 1987.

[Hel88]   M. Held. Computational Geometry for Pocket Machining. In S.M. Slaby and H. Stachel (eds.), *Proc. 3rd Int. Conf. Engineering Graphics and Descriptive Geometry,* p. I:224–231, TU Wien, Austria, July 1988.

[Hel89]   M. Held. GeoPocket – A Sophisticated Computational Geometry Solution of Geometrical and Technological Problems Arising from Pocket Machining. In F. Kimura and A. Rolstadås (eds.), *Proc. Computer Applications in Production and Engineering (CAPE'89),* p. 283–293, North-Holland, Amsterdam, NL, October 1989.

[Hel91]   M. Held. A Geometry-Based Investigation of the Tool Path Generation for Zigzag Pocket Machining. *The Visual Computer,* June 1991.

[Hor79]   R.N. Horspool. *Constructing the Voronoi Diagram in the Plane.* Technical Report SOCS-79.12, McGill U., School of Computer Science, Montreal, Quebec, Canada, July 1979.

[Hos85]   J. Hoschek. Offset Curves in the Plane. *Computer-Aided Design,* 17(2):77–82, March 1985.

[HP84]   M.D. Hall and G. Putnam. An Application of Expert Systems in FMS. In *Proc. CASA/SME AUTOFACT 6 Conf.,* p. 2.26–2.39, Anaheim, CA, USA, October 1984.

[Kir79]   D.G. Kirkpatrick. Efficient Computation of Continuous Skeletons. In *Proc. 20th Annual IEEE Symposium on Foundations of Computer Science,* p. 18–27, 1979.

[Kla83]   R. Klass. An Offset Spline Approximation for Plane Cubic Splines. *Computer-Aided Design,* 15(5):297–299, 1983.

[Kle89]   R. Klein. *Concrete and Abstract Voronoi Diagrams*. Vol. 400 of *Lecture Notes in Computer Science*, Springer-Verlag, 1989. (ISBN 3-540-52055-4).

[Knu68]   D.E. Knuth. *The Art of Computer Programming, Vol. I: Fundamental Algorithms*. Addison-Wesley, Reading, MA, USA, 1968.

[Knu69]   D.E. Knuth. *The Art of Computer Programming, Vol. II: Seminumerical Algorithms*. Addison-Wesley, Reading, MA, USA, 1969.

[Knu73]   D.E. Knuth. *The Art of Computer Programming, Vol. III: Sorting and Searching*. Addison-Wesley, Reading, MA, USA, 1973.

[Knu76]   D.E. Knuth. Big Omicron and Big Omega and Big Theta. *SIGACT News*, 8(2):18–24, April 1976.

[Kra86]   I.H. Kral. *Numerical Control Programming in APT*. Prentice-Hall, Englewood Cliffs, NJ, USA, 1986.

[L*84]   J.B. Lallande et al. Super Pocket. In *Proc. Advancing Manufacturing Technologies*, p. 18–29, Numerical Control Society (NCS), Long Beach, CA, USA, March 1984.

[LD81]   D.T. Lee and R.L. Drysdale. Generalization of Voronoi Diagrams in the Plane. *SIAM Journal of Computing*, 10:73–87, 1981.

[Lee78]   D.T. Lee. *Proximity and Reachability in the Plane*. Technical Report R-831, Coordinated Science Lab, U. of Illinois at Urbana, IL, USA, 1978.

[Lee82]   D.T. Lee. Medial Axis Transformation of a Planar Shape. *IEEE Trans. Pattern Analysis and Machine Intelligence*, PAMI-4(4):363–369, 1982.

[LG87]   U. Langbecker and G. Geise. *Approximation ebener parametrischer Kurven durch Korbbögen (Approximation of Planar Parameterized Curves by Biarcs)*. Technical Report 07-27-87, TU Dresden, Sektion Mathematik, Dresden, FRG, 1987.

[LP84]   D.T. Lee and F.P. Preparata. Computational Geometry - A Survey. *IEEE Trans. Computers*, C-33(12):1072–1101, 1984.

[LS80]   J. Linhart and W. Stegbuchner. *Ausgleichung durch Kreisbögen und Neustationierung in der Straßenvermessung (Adjustment and New Setting by Means of Circular Arcs in the Fields of Road Engineering)*. Technical Report, Inst. für Mathematik, U. Salzburg, Salzburg, Austria, 1980.

[M*84]   R.J. Mayer et al. *Artificial Intelligence - Applications in Manufacturing.* Technical Report, Texas A&M U., College Station, TX, USA, 1984.

[Man88]   M. Mäntylä. *An Introduction to Solid Modeling. Principles of Computer Science Series,* Computer Science Press, Rockville, ML, USA, 1988. (ISBN 0-88175-108-1).

[Meh84a] K. Mehlhorn. *Data Structures and Algorithms, Vol. I: Sorting and Searching. EATCS Monographs on Theoretical Computer Science,* Springer-Verlag, 1984.

[Meh84b] K. Mehlhorn. *Data Structures and Algorithms, Vol. II: Graph Algorithms and NP-Completeness. EATCS Monographs on Theoretical Computer Science,* Springer-Verlag, 1984.

[Meh84c] K. Mehlhorn. *Data Structures and Algorithms, Vol. III: Multidimensional Searching and Computational Geometry. EATCS Monographs on Theoretical Computer Science,* Springer-Verlag, 1984.

[MP69]   M.I. Minski and S. Papert. *Perceptrons.* MIT Press, Cambridge, MA, USA, 1969.

[MP78]   D.E. Muller and F.P. Preparata. Finding the Intersection of Two Convex Polyhedra. *Theoretical Computer Science,* 7(2):217–236, October 1978.

[MP84]   K. Marciniak and B. Putz. Approximation of Spirals by Piecewise Curves of Fewest Circular Arc Segments. *Computer-Aided Design,* 16(2):87–90, March 1984.

[MS87]   S.N. Meshkat and C.M. Sakkas. Voronoi Diagrams for Multiply-Connected Polygonal Domains, II: Implementation and Application. *IBM J. of Research and Development,* 31(3):372–381, May 1987.

[Nil80]   N. Nilsson. *Principles of Artificial Intelligence.* Morgan Kaufmann, Los Altos, CA, USA, and Springer-Verlag, 1980.

[O*84]   T. Ohya et al. Improvements of the Incremental Method for the Voronoi Diagram with Computational Comparison of Various Algorithms. *J. Operations Research Soc. Japan,* 27(4):306–336, 1984.

[OY85]   C. O'Dunlaing and C.K. Yap. A Retraction Method for Planning the Motion of a Disc. *J. of Algorithms,* 6:104–111, 1985.

[Par86]   A. Parkinson. The Use of Solid Models in BUILD as a Database for
           NC Machining. In J.P. Crestin and J.F. McWaters (eds.), *Software
           for Discrete Manufacturing. Prolamat '85*, p. 175–183, North-Holland,
           Amsterdam, NL, June 1986.

[Pau81]   R.P. Paul. *Robot Manipulators: Mathematics, Programming, and Con-
           trol. MIT Press Series in Artificial Intelligence*, MIT Press, Cam-
           bridge, MA, USA, 1981.

[Per]   H. Persson. Private Communication. March 1986 – May 1990.

[Per78]   H. Persson. NC Machining of Arbitrarily Shaped Pockets. *Computer-
           Aided Design*, 10(3):169–174, May 1978.

[PG90]   N.M. Patrikalakis and H.N. Gürsoy. Shape Interrogation by Medial
           Axis Transform. In *Proc. 16th ASME Design Automation Conference*,
           Chicago, September 1990.

[PK83]   K. Preiss and E. Kaplansky. Automatic Mill Routing from Solid Ge-
           ometry Information. In *Proc. Computer Applications in Production
           and Engineering (CAPE'83)*, North-Holland, Amsterdam, NL, 1983.

[PK85]   K. Preiss and E. Kaplansky. Automated CNC Milling by Artificial
           Intelligence Methods. *J. of Manufacturing Systems*, 4(1):51–63, 1985.

[Pre77]   F.P. Preparata. The Medial Axis of a Simple Polygon. In *Proc. 6th
           Symposium on Mathem. Foundations of Computer Science*, p. 443–
           450, 1977.

[Pre89]   K. Preiss. Automated Mill Pocketing Computations. In *Advanced Ge-
           ometric Modeling for Engineering Applications*, North-Holland, Ams-
           terdam, NL, November 1989.

[PS88]   F.P. Preparata and M.I. Shamos. *Computational Geometry - An In-
           troduction. Texts and Monographs in Computer Science*, Springer-
           Verlag, second ed., October 1988. (ISBN 0-540-96131-3).

[Put]   B. Putz. Private Communication. November 1987 – August 1988.

[RD86]   U. Rembold and R. Dillmann. *Computer-Aided Design and Manufac-
           turing. Symbolic Computation - Computer Graphics*, Springer-Verlag,
           1986. (ISBN 0-387-16321-2).

[RR87]   J.R. Rossignac and A.A.G. Requicha. Piecewise-Circular Curves
           for Geometric Modeling. *IBM J. of Research and Development*,
           31(3):296–313, May 1987.

[S*88a] S.E.O. Saeed et al. *An Efficient 2D Solid Offsetting Algorithm.* Technical Report, Dept. of Mechanical Engineering, U. of Leeds, Leeds, UK, 1988.

[S*88b] S.E.O. Saeed et al. Offsetting in Geometric Modeling. *Computer-Aided Design*, 20(2):67–74, March 1988.

[S*88c] G. Spur et al. NC Programming and Dynamic Simulation Based on Solid Models in a CIM Strategy. *Robotics and Computer-Integrated Manufacturing*, 4(3/4):471–481, 1988.

[Sab77] M.A. Sabin. *The Use of Piecewise Forms for the Numerical Representation of Shape.* PhD thesis, Computer and Automation Institute, Hungarian Academy of Sciences, Budapest, Hungary, 1977.

[Sed88] R. Sedgewick. *Algorithms. Computer Science*, Addison-Wesley, Reading, MA, USA, second ed., 1988. (ISBN 0-201-06673-4).

[SH75]   M.I. Shamos and D. Hoey. Closest-Point Problems. In *Proc. 16th Annual IEEE Symposium on Foundations of Computer Science*, October 1975.

[Sha78] M.I. Shamos. *Computational Geometry.* PhD thesis, Dept. of Computer Science, Yale U., New Haven, CT, USA, 1978.

[Sha85] M. Sharir. Intersection and Closest Pair Problems for a Set of Planar Discs. *SIAM Journal of Computing*, 14(2):448–468, May 1985.

[Sha87] T.J. Sharrock. Biarcs in Three Dimensions. In R.R. Martin (ed.), *The Mathematics of Surfaces II*, p. 395–411, Oxford University Press, Oxford, UK, 1987.

[SI89a] K. Sugihara and M. Iri. *Construction of the Voronoi Diagram for One Million Generators in Single-Precision Arithmetic.* Technical Report RMI 89-05, Dept. Mathematical Eng., U. Tokyo, Tokyo 113, Japan, August 1989.

[SI89b] K. Sugihara and M. Iri. *Voronoi2 Reference Manual.* Technical Report RMI 89-04, Dept. Mathematical Eng., U. Tokyo, Tokyo 113, Japan, September 1989.

[SN87]   V. Srinivasan and R. Nackman. Voronoi Diagrams for Multiply-Connected Polygonal Domains, I: Algorithm. *IBM J. of Research and Development*, 31(3):361–372, May 1987.

[Sti88]   S. Stifter. *A Medley of Solutions to the Robot Collision Problem in Two and Three Dimensions.* PhD thesis, Technical Report no. 88-12.0 (RISC-Linz Series), Research Institute for Symbolic Computation, J. Kepler U. Linz, Linz, Austria, 1988.

[TH84]   W. Tiller and E. Hanson. Offsets of Two Dimensional Profiles. *IEEE Computer Graphics and Applications*, 36–46, September 1984.

[Thi11]   A.H. Thiessen. Precipitation Averages for Large Areas. *Monthly Weather Review*, 39:1082–1084, July 1911.

[Tou85]   G.T. Toussaint (ed.). *Computational Geometry.* North-Holland, Amsterdam, NL, 1985.

[Vor08]   G.M. Voronoi. Nouvelles applications des paramètres continus à la théorie des formes quadratiques. Recherches sur les parallélloèdres primitifs. *J. Reine u. Angew. Math.*, 134:198–287, 1908.

[W*87]   H.-P. Wang et al. On the Efficiency of NC Tool Path Planning for Face Milling Operations. *Trans. of the ASME, J. of Engineering for Industry*, 109(4):370–376, November 1987.

[Wir86]   N. Wirth. *Algorithmen und Datenstrukturen mit Modula-2 (Algorithms and Data Structures with Modula-2). Leitfäden und Monographien der Informatik*, B.G. Teubner, Stuttgart, FRG, fourth ed., 1986. (ISBN 3-519-02260-5).

[Wir88]   N. Wirth. *Programming in Modula-2.* Springer-Verlag, fourth ed., 1988. (ISBN 3-540-50150-9).

[Woo86]   J. Woodwark. *Computing Shape.* Butterworths, Guildford, UK, 1986. (ISBN 0-408-01402-4).

[Yap85]   C.K. Yap. *An $O(n * \log n)$ Algorithm for the Voronoi Diagram of a Set of Simple Curve Segments.* Technical Report, Robotics Lab, Courant Institute of Mathematical Sciences, New York U., New York, NY, USA, 1985.

[Yap87]   C.K. Yap. An $O(n * \log n)$ Algorithm for the Voronoi Diagram of a Set of Simple Curve Segments. *Discrete and Computational Geometry*, 2(4):365–393, 1987.

[YY88]   Z. Yeh and D.-N. Ying. An Automated Interface Between CAD and CAM. *Computers and Graphics*, 12(3/4):349–357, 1988.

Lecture Notes in Computer Science

For information about Vols. 1–420
please contact your bookseller or Springer-Verlag

Vol. 421: T. Onodera, S. Kawai, A Formal Model of Visualization in Computer Graphics Systems. X, 100 pages. 1990.

Vol. 422: B. Nebel, Reasoning and Revision in Hybrid Representation Systems. XII, 270 pages. 1990 (Subseries LNAI).

Vol. 423: L.E. Deimel (Ed.), Software Engineering Education. Proceedings, 1990. VI, 164 pages. 1990.

Vol. 424: G. Rozenberg (Ed.), Advances in Petri Nets 1989. VI, 524 pages. 1990.

Vol. 425: C.H. Bergman, R.D. Maddux, D.L. Pigozzi (Eds.), Algebraic Logic and Universal Algebra in Computer Science. Proceedings, 1988. XI, 292 pages. 1990.

Vol. 426: N. Houbak, SIL – a Simulation Language. VII, 192 pages. 1990.

Vol. 427: O. Faugeras (Ed.), Computer Vision – ECCV 90. Proceedings, 1990. XII, 619 pages. 1990.

Vol. 428: D. Bjørner, C.A.R. Hoare, H. Langmaack (Eds.), VDM '90. VDM and Z – Formal Methods in Software Development. Proceedings, 1990. XVII, 580 pages. 1990.

Vol. 429: A. Miola (Ed.), Design and Implementation of Symbolic Computation Systems. Proceedings, 1990. XII, 284 pages. 1990.

Vol. 430: J.W. de Bakker, W.-P. de Roever, G. Rozenberg (Eds.), Stepwise Refinement of Distributed Systems. Models, Formalisms, Correctness. Proceedings, 1989. X, 808 pages. 1990.

Vol. 431: A. Arnold (Ed.), CAAP '90. Proceedings, 1990. VI, 285 pages. 1990.

Vol. 432: N. Jones (Ed.), ESOP '90. Proceedings, 1990. IX, 436 pages. 1990.

Vol. 433: W. Schröder-Preikschat, W. Zimmer (Eds.), Progress in Distributed Operating Systems and Distributed Systems Management. Proceedings, 1989. V, 206 pages. 1990.

Vol. 434: J.-J. Quisquater, J. Vandewalle (Eds.), Advances in Cryptology – EUROCRYPT '89. Proceedings, 1989. X, 710 pages. 1990.

Vol. 435: G. Brassard (Ed.), Advances in Cryptology – CRYPTO '89. Proceedings, 1989. XIII, 634 pages. 1990.

Vol. 436: B. Steinholtz, A. Sølvberg, L. Bergman (Eds.), Advanced Information Systems Engineering. Proceedings, 1990. X, 392 pages. 1990.

Vol. 437: D. Kumar (Ed.), Current Trends in SNePS – Semantic Network Processing System. Proceedings, 1989. VII, 162 pages. 1990. (Subseries LNAI).

Vol. 438: D.H. Norrie, H.W. Six (Eds.), Computer Assisted Learning – ICCAL '90. Proceedings, 1990. VII, 467 pages. 1990.

Vol. 439: P. Gorny, M. Tauber (Eds.), Visualization in Human-Computer Interaction. Proceedings, 1988. VI, 274 pages. 1990.

Vol. 440: E. Börger, H. Kleine Büning, M.M. Richter (Eds.), CSL '89. Proceedings, 1989. VI, 437 pages. 1990.

Vol. 441: T. Ito, R.H. Halstead, Jr. (Eds.), Parallel Lisp: Languages and Systems. Proceedings, 1989. XII, 364 pages. 1990.

Vol. 442: M. Main, A. Melton, M. Mislove, D. Schmidt (Eds.), Mathematical Foundations of Programming Semantics. Proceedings, 1989. VI, 439 pages. 1990.

Vol. 443: M.S. Paterson (Ed.), Automata, Languages and Programming. Proceedings, 1990. IX, 781 pages. 1990.

Vol. 444: S. Ramani, R. Chandrasekar, K.S.R. Anjaneyulu (Eds.), Knowledge Based Computer Systems. Proceedings, 1989. X, 546 pages. 1990. (Subseries LNAI).

Vol. 445: A.J.M. van Gasteren, On the Shape of Mathematical Arguments. VIII, 181 pages. 1990.

Vol. 446: L. Plümer, Termination Proofs for Logic Programs. VIII, 142 pages. 1990. (Subseries LNAI).

Vol. 447: J.R. Gilbert, R. Karlsson (Eds.), SWAT '90. 2nd Scandinavian Workshop on Algorithm Theory. Proceedings, 1990. VI, 417 pages. 1990.

Vol. 448: B. Simons, A. Spector (Eds.), Fault Tolerant Distributed Computing. VI, 298 pages. 1990.

Vol. 449: M.E. Stickel (Ed.), 10th International Conference on Automated Deduction. Proceedings, 1990. XVI, 688 pages. 1990. (Subseries LNAI).

Vol. 450: T. Asano, T. Ibaraki, H. Imai, T. Nishizeki (Eds.), Algorithms. Proceedings, 1990. VIII, 479 pages. 1990.

Vol. 451: V. Marík, O. Stepánková, Z. Zdráhal (Eds.), Artificial Intelligence in Higher Education. Proceedings, 1989. IX, 247 pages. 1990. (Subseries LNAI).

Vol. 452: B. Rovan (Ed.), Mathematical Foundations of Computer Science 1990. Proceedings, 1990. VIII, 544 pages. 1990.

Vol. 453: J. Seberry, J. Pieprzyk (Eds.), Advances in Cryptology – AUSCRYPT '90 Proceedings, 1990. IX. 462 pages. 1990.

Vol. 454: V. Diekert, Combinatorics on Traces. XII, 165 pages. 1990.

Vol. 455: C.A. Floudas, P.M. Pardalos, A Collection of Test Problems for Constrained Global Optimization Algorithms. XIV, 180 pages. 1990.

Vol. 456: P. Deransart, J. Maluszyn´ski (Eds.), Programming Language Implementation and Logic Programming. Proceedings, 1990. VIII, 401 pages. 1990.

Vol. 457: H. Burkhart (Ed.), CONPAR '90 – VAPP IV. Proceedings, 1990. XIV, 900 pages. 1990.

Vol. 458: J.C.M. Baeten, J.W. Klop (Eds.), CONCUR '90. Proceedings, 1990. VII, 537 pages. 1990.

Vol. 459: R. Studer (Ed.), Natural Language and Logic. Proceedings, 1989. VII, 252 pages. 1990. (Subseries LNAI).

Vol. 460: J. Uhl, H.A. Schmid, A Systematic Catalogue of Reusable Abstract Data Types. XII, 344 pages. 1990.

Vol. 461: P. Deransart, M. Jourdan (Eds.), Attribute Grammars and their Applications. Proceedings, 1990. VIII, 358 pages. 1990.

Vol. 462: G. Gottlob, W. Nejdl (Eds.), Expert Systems in Engineering. Proceedings, 1990. IX, 260 pages. 1990. (Subseries LNAI).

Vol. 463: H. Kirchner, W. Wechler (Eds.), Algebraic and Logic Programming. Proceedings, 1990. VII, 386 pages. 1990.